Your First Year in Code

A complete guide for new & aspiring developers

Isaac Lyman

Your First Year in Code

A complete guide for new & aspiring developers

Isaac Lyman

ISBN 9780578564999

Leanpub

Contents

Foreword

Your first year in code is a whirlwind, I know it was for me. The more you learn, the more you learn that there's more to learn. Code is such an abstract problem that there's no set of always-applicable rules or rock-solid advice. Code powers the planet these days, but knowledge is still passed down through our elders and cultivated via community.

There is no one true way to be a coder. Gone are the days, if ever they truly existed, of the archetypal "programmer." We all carry supercomputers in our pockets. Cloud service outages are front page news; email servers and encryption can be everyday political topics. The nerds have won and code has become mainstream.

The only way for code to be *for* the people is if it is created *by* the people. We cannot let this craft become magic wielded by a select few. We must ensure that the discourse is accessible to all.

The fact that this book is such a true bottom-up community initiative speaks to the soul of the material. Isaac and the rest of the incredible authors assembled in these pages represent the warmth, humanity, and diversity of our industry. If you are in your first year of code, you're lucky to have discovered material like this. I wish I had. It's still a tremendous read years into my career.

Happy coding!

Ben Halpern

Founder, The DEV Community

dev.to/ben

About the editor

I'm a self-taught programmer.

By that I mean a lot of different people taught me to code. Mostly strangers. When I was in middle school, I found an ebook called *C++ For Dummies* that my brother had bought. I read it until the chapter on pointers, where I got confused and gave up. Then a few months later I did it again. I read the first several chapters of that book over and over until I practically knew them by heart. I wrote a Fahrenheit-to-Celsius converter. I started thinking about classes and objects. I was so curious.

Part of that curiosity stemmed from the fact that I *identified* with code. Computer programming was nerdy, and I was a nerd. I mean, I had friends who wore Naruto headbands and played Yu-Gi-Oh! in the cafeteria, and I wasn't quite *that* nerdy. But by my senior year of high school I was president of the computer support team and co-president of the speech and debate team, so that should tell you what kind of kid I was. Code was exactly the kind of thing I wanted to play with.

Anyway, I learned Python a year or two after I first picked up that C++ book, and then a bit of HTML, and then Visual Basic, and before long I had filled up a folder on my family's computer with ebooks and CHM files (an old form of hyperlinked documentation) that all had ridiculous titles like *Learn PHP in 24 Hours*. I had even written a couple of programs on my TI-84 calculator to save time on calculus homework. But I had also written off computer programming as an unrealistic career ambition. Back then coding just seemed like a fun hobby for a kid who didn't get out much. I had no way of knowing that over the next decade Silicon Valley would explode with tech startups, web developers would command salaries comparable to corporate lawyers, cell phone apps would become a 100 billion dollar market, and nerds would take over the world.

So I set a more attainable career goal: become a business lawyer, then a politician. And that'd be the whole story if I hadn't run out of money during my sophomore year of college. After a disappointing job search, I managed to land a position as a technical support agent, fixing printers and upgrading operating systems in a cubicle on the outskirts of campus. And on the days when all the computers were working and the printers were attending to their queues, I was learning JavaScript. The first version of my personal website, isaaclyman.com[1], was built almost entirely during downtime on that job. And I have that first website to thank for the career I have now.

I love this career, and I'm happy to report that I've been cured of all my former political ambitions. I'm now a senior software engineer at a billion-dollar company that helps hospitals save lives through cutting-edge healthcare analytics. I didn't know it was possible to have this much fun at work. But coding *is* fun, and I think that's the first thing I want to say about it: for all the negatives in this field of work (and there are a few), I still get a thrill whenever I write a clever piece of code.

Looking back on my career, it's clear that I've had an extraordinary amount of privilege on my side. Tech is full of gatekeepers, unwritten rules, poor documentation, and unacknowledged bias.

---

[1]http://isaaclyman.com

Sometimes it seems that everywhere you look, there's someone else telling you you're "not a real developer" unless you're exactly like them. Many talented programmers have been squeezed out by these institutional problems. It will take a generation's combined efforts to fix them, but in the meantime, I hope this book can make a difference. In its pages are the encouraging and persistent voices of your colleagues, telling you that you can do this, you're smart enough, others have been where you are, and we're all in it together. My co-authors and I have done our best to write the tech industry's unwritten rules, call attention to its blind spots, share the knowledge we wish we'd had years ago, and open the gates.

I hope this book is useful to you. If you have questions about anything you read here or just want to say hello, you can drop me a line on Twitter (@isaacdlyman).

Good luck!

Isaac Lyman

About this book

It all started with a question: what do you wish you had known during your first year as a programmer? I asked this question online when I announced the book, and before I knew it almost a hundred software developers from around the world had volunteered to help me answer it. Some signed up as beta readers and others offered to write content. The whole thing came together at an incredible pace. In the end, the work of 15 other authors was selected for inclusion. The following chapters represent some of the best, most practical advice the development community has to offer. The author of each chapter is listed underneath the title.

The goal of this book is to help you start your programming journey a year or two ahead of where we were when we started. There's a lot of how-to, a splash of career advice, and a bit of pep talk. It's a good read for Computer Science majors, dev bootcamp students, beginning devs on a self-learning path, or anyone who wants to figure out if programming is for them.

More importantly, this is stuff you won't easily find elsewhere. You won't get it in a college course or a bootcamp. It won't be in the company manual for your first job. Most software books are extremely technical; this one is different. It will apply to you regardless of what sector or programming language you want to get into. It's mostly about the squishy stuff: what happens around and outside the code. This is important because writing code is only a small part of a programmer's job—researchers have[2] found[3] that the average programmer only writes about 25 lines of code per day. Code is really just the beginning.

So what do programmers actually do? They go to meetings. They draw diagrams. They learn. They get stuck. They bang their heads on their desks. They help their teammates solve problems. They wade through an ocean of self-doubt. They field messages from tech recruiters. They update their resumes and negotiate for remote work options. They balance their three-month-old baby on one knee and a book about C++ on the other. They think methodically and ask questions nobody else has thought about.

These things aren't code, and in many ways they're more important than code. They're what this book is about. And it's about you: your career, your journey, all the amazing options that will open up to you as you learn to code.

The book is not cumulative; each chapter stands on its own, so read them in any order you like. We've done our best to keep things simple and avoid jargon, but if you encounter an unfamiliar term, you can refer to Appendix A for a definition.

Whoever you are, we're excited that you're here. We have the highest of hopes for you. And we hope you enjoy *Your First Year in Code*.

---

[2]https://blogs.msdn.microsoft.com/philipsu/2006/06/14/broken-windows-theory/
[3]https://dzone.com/articles/programmer-productivity

Introduction: Code is the best, code is the worst

Isaac Lyman

Code is the best

Coding is an act of pure creation. It's often exhilarating: you type a sequence of words into the void and, assuming you don't mess up, entire worlds begin to exist. Software development is one of the few fields where you can create something of extraordinary value without expending any raw materials. In a way, coding more closely resembles the TV stereotype of witches and wizards than the TV stereotype of coders (or developers, or engineers, or whatever they call themselves—see my chapter "Choosing a job title" for more on that topic).

There are moments as a software engineer when you know exactly what you're doing. You come into a project, see a problem you've solved before, and every component of the solution springs into your mind. Suddenly you are a being of unstoppable force; you are elemental. You are typing as fast as you can, everything is working perfectly, every piece is elegant. You hand off the finished product and take in the admiration of your peers. It's a triumph.

There are other times where you come up against a challenge you don't have the first idea how to solve. And this makes you happy too, because learning is fun. You start exploring, surfing Q&A sites, reading the 11th page of old forum threads, copying snippets, compiling and debugging code, and before you know it you've figured it out. You tuck the solution safely away in your mind for next time. You can't wait to do it again.

In the right environment, code is the ultimate brain teaser. Every last scrap of intelligence, creativity, determination, quirkiness, playfulness, intuition—none of it goes to waste when you're writing code. You get so close to your own potential that you feel like you could reach out and touch it. That's not to say you'll always be recognized for it, but it's satisfying in and of itself.

Programming is a science, as we all know. But it's also an art. Like the painter who imagines beautiful sun-dappled landscapes, or the musician who wakes up whistling a tune, many programmers find their imagination filling up with code. They daydream of apps and libraries. Their GitHub profiles are full of projects that never got finished, but only because they were so eager to start on something else. Not everyone is so obsessed—you certainly don't *need* to be to have a successful career in code—but everybody is here for something, even if it's just the salary and benefits. And whatever your reason is, there's a place for you.

Code is the worst

Coding can be a real headache.

There's a well-known cycle to fixing bugs. You examine the problem; you make a guess about what might be causing it; you update the code based on your theory; you test the new code; if the problem isn't fixed, you start over. Sometimes this goes on for hours. Sometimes for days. Sometimes until it just doesn't seem worth it anymore.

In the best of circumstances, you'll be on a team of compassionate and attentive people. They'll listen to you and make tactful suggestions. You'll take their ideas back to your computer and ride a wave of genius all the way to your next task. Your boss will drop by your office afterward to tell you what a great job you did. You'll go home at 4:30 and spend the evening relaxing at home.

You don't always get to work in the best of circumstances. Someday you may find yourself struggling to concentrate in an open floor plan office, sharing a desk with eight other programmers, drowning in noise from phone calls and water-cooler conversations. The company will expect you to work 16-hour days if you're not meeting their deadlines, which they never consulted you about in the first place. Your manager will think coding is black magic. Your teammates won't seem to think you belong in tech, and some of them will have never learned how to hold a polite conversation. Some days will be a nightmare of egotistical managers, unreadable error messages, burnout and anxiety.

Sometimes you'll wonder if you chose the wrong career.

Code is just a tool

The truth is, most of the time coding isn't amazing. And most of the time it isn't miserable. Code is a means to an end, and the ups and downs of your career will be more about people than about lines of code.

For now other people will decide what you build, who's on your team, and whether you feel emotionally safe at the office. But you've still got a few responsibilities. To be a good teammate—to say things like "you belong here" and "it's okay to make mistakes" and "you deserve a break." To break stereotypes about programmers being insensitive and rude. To have the courage to quit if your boss doesn't treat you or your teammates well.

Later on, you'll be the one making decisions. Code will be the best on some days and the worst on others, and it'll be because of you. You'll set the tone for an entire team or department or company.

We're trusting you to do the right thing.

Different learning pathways into tech

Clifford Fajardo

There are many industries (law, medicine, etc.) where a formal credential is required before you begin work in the field. By contrast, the software development field, like many creative fields (business, art, etc.), does not require that you have a formal credential to start working in the field. Given this fact, there are different learning pathways you can take to reach your goal of becoming a professional software developer.

In the pages that follow, I'll outline the learning path I took to become a professional software developer. I'll start off by sharing how I began programming, then cover my self-learning path, coding bootcamp path, and university path, then circle back to the self-learning path I'm on now. My aim is to shed light on the thought process I used to inform which learning path to embark on, based on my circumstances, and ultimately demonstrate that there are several paths you can choose.

The night I discovered code

It was mid-December. I had just finished a semester of classes at my community college, and now I had two weeks of vacation before the beginning of the new year. On one of these evenings, while browsing the web as usual, I discovered a free learn-to-code website called codecademy.com. A few short minutes into using the site, I made a blue box with HTML and CSS. A few minutes later I made an alert box pop up on my screen with the message, "Hello Clifford." I was astonished that I had just made my computer bring an idea to life before my eyes. Thus began my journey into the world of software development and teaching myself how to code.

The path of self-learning

After discovering codecademy.com, I continued learning the fundamentals of web development whenever I had free time after work or class.

In 2016, halfway through my second year of college, I had been teaching myself to code for almost a year. At that point I became curious about this hobby of coding I had picked up and naively started doing research online to see if programming was something I could do full time as a job. To my surprise it was, and in my research I stumbled upon some coding bootcamps. I found out that this was an alternative learning path to a traditional college degree.

After this discovery, I started following the blogs of several bootcamps and the blogs of their students who were sharing their experiences. Despite the excitement I had about bootcamps at the time, I continued teaching myself web programming, kept the idea of attending a bootcamp as a possibility in the back of my mind, and continued through college.

My decision between college and a coding bootcamp

When April 2016 came around, I had completed my general education requirements at community college and my college transfer letters came in. I was fortunate enough to receive full scholarships to study Sociology at UC Berkeley and many other flagship state colleges. Despite this accomplishment, I knew deep down that I wanted to pursue computer programming. More specifically, I knew front-end software engineering was what I enjoyed and wanted to focus on.

I had a decision to make. I was conflicted about which path to take so I asked myself: Do you want to spend two more years as a transfer student to complete the remaining half of your undergraduate degree, studying something you're no longer enthusiastic about? Or would it be better to pursue your dream now and maximize your personal growth and development?

I decided to make a seemingly risky but nonetheless well-calculated decision based on my circumstances: to put my formal education on hold and do the Hack Reactor coding bootcamp, an immersive 12-week course. Choosing Hack Reactor, I would later come to realize, was one of the best decisions I had ever made in my life.

Why I chose a bootcamp

The bootcamp approach made the most of my circumstances. I didn't want to switch majors and be in a classroom for another four years, despite having had a fantastic experience in college. Instead, I felt I could be gaining years of work experience, problem-solving skills, and personal growth, all while getting paid to learn and earning income for my family.

I considered continuing on the self-learning pathway. However, I felt I could accelerate my learning by being around other highly motivated peers and following a rigorous curriculum, which I probably wouldn't have had the courage to tackle alone at that time. Ultimately I wanted to obtain a high degree of competency quicker, in a more structured environment, and kickstart my career.

Truthfully, another major factor that influenced my decision was the fact that I was tired of struggling financially and living under the poverty line. I was tired of seeing my twin brother and my parents, a janitor and a physically disabled stay-at-home mom, under financial strain. If I had chosen to go major in computer science given my circumstances, I would still be finishing my last year of college right now and my family would still be struggling, which is no longer the case.

Though I did have to combat thoughts about being a "dropout," I believed I could break into the software industry. Market conditions in my area were favorable (they generally still are across the United States) and there was plenty of evidence and testimony that I could start a fantastic career as a software developer without a degree, since thousands of other bootcamp graduates had done so before me.

"Why didn't you just change your major to computer science (CS) at community college?"

Changing my major to CS would have meant staying another 2 - 2.5 more years at my community college and taking several classes merely to complete prerequisites so I could qualify for the CS major at the universities I was applying to.

Another consideration was that all of the colleges I was applying to transfer to didn't offer a curriculum covering the topics I was most interested in. I wanted to take courses where I could learn about web applications, JavaScript and NodeJS, front-end web development, and responsive design.

> "Why didn't you change your major to computer science (CS) at the four-year university, UC Berkeley?"

I wouldn't have been able to switch my major to CS without taking all the pre-requisite classes for the major. Again, that would have meant two more years of classes just to qualify for the major. On top of that, after qualifying, I would need another two years' worth of upper division credits to graduate. This meant it would take me four more years of school before obtaining a degree and my first full-time entry-level job. The idea of spending four more years in large classrooms worrying about my grades and studying a wide array of topics that weren't immediately relevant to my goals didn't resonate with me.

In summary, I chose the bootcamp for three main reasons: (1) To get to my goal sooner by being in a structured, immersive learning environment; (2) To support my family; and (3) To study the areas of software development that I wanted, which weren't offered at colleges in my area.

After beginning my career as a software engineer at Salesforce in San Francisco, I attended a semester at UC Berkeley as a working student and took one of their most popular computer sciences classes. I had the opportunity to experience what it was like to study computer science in a college setting, and it validated what I felt previously. I preferred learning environments where I had more flexibility to choose what to learn and where I didn't need to worry about grades. Although the college path wasn't for me, for many people the college path is excellent and offers a lot of value.

A high-level overview of coding bootcamps

Coding bootcamps are immersive technical coding schools that teach the essential programming skills and technologies that employers seek.

In terms of curriculum and learning structure, not all bootcamps are the same. Some are in-person, others are online; the majority require a full-time commitment while others are part-time. The goals and curriculum of each coding bootcamp may be different as well. For example, there are bootcamps that focus on mobile development, data science, machine learning, full-stack web development, and so on.

A few more considerations about bootcamps are:

- Instruction: There are bootcamps that help people with very little or almost no coding experience get to a job-ready stage. In contrast, some coding bootcamps require candidates to have a minimum of a few months of self-study experience and meet a specific technical bar via an admissions test. Most coding bootcamps require admitted students to complete pre-course material before starting the program. This ensures every student is beginning with nearly the same baseline knowledge and helps maximize the content that can be covered in the program's few months.

- Quality: Generally, the more rigorous the admissions standards are, the higher the quality of instruction, curriculum, students, alumni network and job success outcomes.
- Alumni networks: Generally, the longer a bootcamp has been around, the more alumni you have access to. For example, I'm part of an alumni network of several thousand graduates who are working across nearly every subset of the software development industry. As a new graduate or an experienced alumnus, this may be helpful since you have a large pool of people you can connect with.
- Price: The tuition varies for each bootcamp. Many programs allow you to put down a small down payment (or nothing at all) and pay back the rest of the program fee once you secure a job as a software developer.
- The job hunt after the program: Similar to colleges that may have a career center to help guide and support students in their job hunt, most bootcamps offer that as well. It's important to note that if you are coming into a bootcamp with the expectation that a job will be handed to you after you graduate or that it's the bootcamp's responsibility to find you jobs, that's not the reality. You should leverage all of the resources that your bootcamp has to offer to maximize your odds.
- How long it takes to obtain a job: Some of your peers will find jobs much faster than others, due to varying circumstances. For example, it took me two and a half months of studying and job hunting every day to secure my first software developer job, but it may be different for you.

I want to highlight that bootcamps are not for everyone. It's essential to evaluate your own goals and learning style and make the choice that meets your needs best.

The cost of forsaking a computer science degree

It's important to briefly address a few points concerning the cost of forsaking a computer science degree, as to avoid any surprises:

- You will be competing for the same jobs that computer science graduates are applying for. You will need to work hard to demonstrate that you have what it takes to do the job and have the ability to fill any knowledge gaps for a role.
- It may be harder to initially demonstrate to employers the value you bring without a formal credential. However, do not be discouraged. The good news is many (perhaps most) employers nowadays have progressive hiring practices and will consider anyone who has the skills required for the role and who they feel is a good match.
- Some jobs and employers require a computer science degree, which is fair given that every employer has different needs.

- Often, as a bootcamper or self-learner, you won't get the broad exposure to software (operating systems, compilers, distributed systems, etc.) that most computer science graduates obtain. Some may doubt the importance of this; however, no one can dispute that knowing more about what exists and what tools are available to you is beneficial. Of course, you can always fill in gaps in knowledge if you're deliberate about your learning.

Differences between bootcamps, colleges and self-taught pathways

Below is a brief overview of the differences and similarities between the different learning paths discussed in this chapter. At the end of this chapter, additional resources are provided for those who would like more information.

Time Commitment

- Bootcamp: 3-9 months; varies depending on the bootcamp.
- College: 4 years; varies depending on the college or individual.
- Self-Taught: varies depending on the individual and whether they are studying part-time or full-time. Some people qualify for a development job in a few months, others may take several months and others a year or more.

Financial Cost

- Bootcamp: Varies depending on the reputation and duration of the program. Most immersive bootcamps range from $9,000 - $20,000 USD.
- College: Varies depending on the college, reputation and duration of the program. According to a 2019 statistical report on the average cost of a 4-year college in the United States:
  - Public 4-year college: ~$20,000 / year (assuming no financial aid or help at all). Subtract ~$11,000 if you are living at home.
  - Private 4-year college: ~$46,950 / year. Subtract ~$11,000 if you are living at home.
- Self-Taught: Cost varies depending on the courses and resources you purchase. It's possible to obtain most or all of the information you need for free, online or with a library card. Some libraries have partnerships with paid services (e.g. Treehouse or LinkedIn Learning).

Learning Curriculum

- Bootcamp: Shorter length programs (~12 weeks) focus on a very specialized curriculum to help students develop expertise in only a few technologies. This tradeoff is intentional, as most bootcamps assume and trust that their graduates will continue learning the necessary skills they need throughout their career. Longer programs, like the Lambda School which is 9 months long, not only teach highly marketable technologies but also do their best to bridge the gap between the exposure computer science majors typically obtain and what shorter bootcamps often don't cover.

- College: Given that there is more time to cover material, computer science graduates tend to have a much broader view of the entire field of programming, especially when it comes to theory. As one computer science graduate, Christian Charukiewicz, puts it:

Personally, as someone who has just finished their CS degree, I can tell you that I feel like my learning has only begun. I think one of the most valuable aspects of my degree is that it has lifted many of the "unknown unknowns" and turned them into "known unknowns." That means I may not be an expert in compilers, or system programming, or CS theory, or any of the topics I studied in college. However, I know that they are out there, and I know what most of them are so that I can research them and hone my skills as needed as my career progresses.

- Self-Taught: With freedom comes a great deal of responsibility. You will need to dedicate lots of time to curating your own learning material and continuously evaluate the quality of the resources you are consuming, as opposed to a college student or bootcamper who is following a structured learning curriculum. For the highly dedicated learner, being in complete control of one's education can be a source of great satisfaction. On the flip side, it's easier to consciously or unconsciously neglect learning topics that may be essential for your growth, since there is less guidance. You don't know what you don't know.

Networking and Cultural Growth

- Bootcamp: The majority of my peers already had years of professional experience and degrees in other industries, as many bootcampers are transitioning between careers. Bootcampers can leverage their past experience to help them obtain new opportunities in the software field. For example, I have a friend who was a DJ/audio engineer before becoming a programmer. He went on to work for a music streaming company after bootcamp.
- College: Typically younger aged peers, 18-25, without full-time work experience. Colleges usually offer internships, volunteer opportunities, and projects for students to gain practical experience.
- Self-Taught: There's no built-in network when you're self-taught, so you'll need to rely on jobs, meetups, conferences, open-source projects, social media, and other self-driven forms of outreach in order to build your network.

Similarities: bootcamps & college

Networking and Cultural Growth

- Your peers, instructors and alumni network are easily accessible since you typically see them daily. This translates into having people close by to quickly learn and expand your worldview from, not just in programming.

Job Support

- Nearly all bootcamps and colleges have a career or job resources center for students and alumni; they have a vested interest in your success. After all, what institution wouldn't want to showcase their graduates succeeding?

Learning Curriculum

- The material you are learning has been evaluated and selected by others. Thus, you can spend your energy on learning, instead of hand-curating your learning resources.

Additional resources

- Teach Yourself Computer Science[4] - An opinionated guide to Computer Science learning for self-taught devs and bootcamp grads.
- CourseReport: Coding Bootcamp Cost Comparison[5] - A list of coding bootcamps in the United States and how much they cost.
- Average Cost of College in America: 2019 Report[6] - An overview of the full cost of college attendance in the United States.
- Coding Bootcamp vs. Computer Science Degree[7] - An infographic comparing several aspects of college degrees and development bootcamps.
- Bootcamps vs. College[8] - A comparison of bootcamp and college grads from the perspective of a company that specializes in developer job placement.
- Would you choose a coding bootcamp or a computer science related degree? Why?[9] - A collection of differing opinions on whether a bootcamp or college degree is the better choice.
- Treehouse for Libraries[10] - Information on the availability of Treehouse's software development courses through your local library.
- The Odin Project[11] - A course in web development for self-taught developers.

---

[4]https://teachyourselfcs.com/
[5]https://www.coursereport.com/blog/coding-bootcamp-cost-comparison-full-stack-immersives
[6]https://www.valuepenguin.com/student-loans/average-cost-of-college
[7]https://www.whatsthehost.com/coding-bootcamp-vs-cs-degree/
[8]https://triplebyte.com/blog/bootcamps-vs-college
[9]https://www.quora.com/Would-you-choose-a-coding-bootcamp-or-a-computer-science-related-degree-Why
[10]https://join.teamtreehouse.com/libraries/
[11]https://www.theodinproject.com/

How (not) to learn

Vlad Levin

Image licensed by Pixabay[12]

When I was younger, I remember having some odd ideas about what it meant to learn. In particular, I recall that I thought learning meant reading a textbook very diligently from beginning to end. I would even read the foreword. Maybe that was just me! Now I look back and wonder why I had such strange and unproductive notions.

However, I think the education system at every level does tend to suffer from problems that prevent people from learning effectively: students are shepherded through too many subjects at a time and learn the material in a linear and rote manner. As a result, I think it's not uncommon for people to promptly forget much of what they "learned" in school, including at colleges and universities, as soon as they pass their exams.

The following are some heuristics I've built up over time which have helped me when I'm learning something new. If you have the luxury of learning something on your own, consider trying these out. Even if you're in school, I hope some of these ideas may be of help if you actually care about learning instead of just getting through the classes.

---

[12]https://pixabay.com/es/illustrations/narrativa-la-historia-sue%C3%B1o-decir-794978/

Build intuition

With almost any technical subject, it's easy to get involved in all of the complicated details. Doing so prematurely can be a bad idea though. If we don't understand the broader context, those technical details can quickly overwhelm us.

When you're first reading about a given topic, try to grasp the big picture. Why is this important or useful? How does it fit with other topics or technologies? What's the problem that it's trying to solve? Is there another way to look at this? Answering questions like these will give you a perspective that will help motivate a deeper understanding as you dig into the more technical details.

Building intuition is a gradual process. Often clues can be found sprinkled through a given book or other source of information. Keep an eye out for the clues and use them to build up a picture in your mind of the high level principles and connections. Always keep asking yourself: "What's the big idea here?"

Intuition is something everyone works on, from novices to experts. As a novice programmer, I remember learning C for the first time. At first I had difficulty understanding the starting and ending conditions of `for` loops, e.g. `for (int i=0; i<length; i++)`. I distinctly remember making notes in a notepad, manually tracking the value of `i`, as well as sketching an array with arrows pointing to the current index during and after each iteration. Eventually it became second-nature, but I still remember that it wasn't obvious to me in the beginning.

Later on, I used similar strategies to get familiar with increasingly complex recursive algorithms. I would work through small examples manually. Again, I drew small sketches, showing everything on the stack before and after each recursive call. This helped me to internalize what was really going on with a given algorithm.

Here's another real-world example of building intuition: fairly recently I needed to look up the formula for standard deviation in statistics. It wasn't my first time using it, but this time I suddenly noticed that part of the formula looked a lot like the Pythagorean theorem. That had never occurred to me before. I was able to work out that the standard deviation can be thought of geometrically, in terms of the distance between two points. This was very exciting for me. Before, I had always taken the formula for granted, as a black box. I knew how to use it, but I didn't know why the equation was what it was. Afterward, I felt that I understood it much better. I could visualize what was happening, and I knew that from now on, it would be easy for me to derive the formula from scratch.

Once something becomes intuitive, you can visualize it, you know when it applies and how it works, without needing to consciously think about it.

Knowledge debt

In the same way that there's financial debt and technical debt, there's also knowledge debt. If we're faced with something we don't understand, often the temptation is to move ahead anyway, hoping it won't bite us later. In fact, sometimes that's okay. Maybe an in-depth understanding isn't necessary— we just need to get a specific thing done. Or maybe going further into the material will elucidate the point we're stuck on right now.

Both of these things can be true at times, but it's not a good approach to leave behind such gaps as a matter of course. It will cause the foundations of our knowledge to get more and more shaky. Eventually, that's precisely what will stall progress completely. For instance, a lot of people think math is "too hard." I believe the reason is that they kept being pushed along in school to more advanced topics, but all the while they were leaving more and more loose ends behind.

Any technical subject, including math, computer science, and programming, requires effort (at least for us mortals), but if you take it one step at a time, and you make sure to master the individual steps along the way, you can go a lot further than you might think.

PDL: Problem-Driven Learning

Just as test-driven development (TDD, see below) is about writing code to satisfy a measurable criterion—making a test pass—I like applying the same notion to learning. Learning can seem like a passive process of osmosis. However, we're fooling ourselves if we think we understand that way. It's okay to read something lightly to get a broad overview of a topic, but if we really want to understand how to apply our knowledge, *we should make the learning a result of solving problems.* This is the best way to make the leap from theory to practice.

We can start with a simple problem and learn just enough to solve it, kind of like making a test pass in TDD. Moving on to a similar, maybe slightly harder problem, can we solve it without doing any extra reading? If so, great. Otherwise, we go back over our material to find what we need. This makes our reading much more active and goal-oriented.

The more problems we can solve and the more diverse those problems are, the stronger and more concrete our understanding becomes. This is the only real measure of how well we understand something.

> **What is TDD?** Test-Driven Development, or TDD, is a practice that's used to improve the quality of new code. The idea is to develop functionality in small steps. Each step starts with a *unit test* (see Appendix A, "Automated test" and "Unit test"). Each test has 3 parts. The first part describes the initial conditions for the test. The second part describes the action to be taken by the test. The third part describes the changes that are expected as a result of the action.
>
> After you've written a test, you start things off by running it. It's good practice to run a test before you actually implement the behavior described in the test. Therefore, a brand new unit test should generally fail when you run it for the very first time. Once you've demonstrated that the test initially fails, you fill in the code that the test is targeting. Having done this, you can confirm your code works correctly by running the test again. This time it should pass. The last step is called *refactoring*. The idea is to look at the code you've written to make the test pass and to clean it up. This is your opportunity to remove duplicate logic and to clarify the naming of things like classes, functions, variables, etc. Basically you can reorganize your code however you wish as long as the expected behavior doesn't change. Once you're done refactoring, you can run the test once more to

make sure that it still passes. Unit tests are helpful when you're initially developing a piece of functionality, but they're also useful in *regression*. That means you can periodically run your entire test suite, say before committing your code to your repository. If anything you've done breaks older tests, that alerts you to the possibility that you've introduced bugs with your latest code, and gives you a chance to fix those bugs first. Making sure all of the tests pass before checking in is a good practice. It gives you additional confidence that your code is still all working properly.

Multiple sources of truth

Reading a single textbook or article is often a bad idea. Any source of information will be written in a particular context. It will skip some steps and also make assumptions about what you know. If you're confused (and even if you're not!), it's good to look for additional sources.

If the material you're reading seems too advanced, look for more beginner-friendly treatments. If you're reading about something in a particular programming language and it is not making sense, try to find the same topic addressed in a language you're more familiar with. Maybe what you're currently reading is too technical. In that case, look for high level descriptions to build intuition about the subject. In that regard, I really like the idea of ExplainLikeImFive[13], a tag used online for articles that explain complex topics very simply.

Fewer subjects at a time

I've talked to a lot of graduates from schools in many fields about their experiences, including math, science, medicine, dentistry, etc. Often enough, it's the same story: Learn by memorization, pass the exam, forget most of it, and repeat. I don't think it's the students' fault either. Students are loaded with so many classes to take each semester that it's very hard to do even a halfway decent job of learning. I think this is true in pretty much every field of study, and it's certainly true in computer science.

For most people, I think that cutting down the number of courses and focussing on fundamentals would be much better. When a student completes a class, it should mean they have mastered the material. The same idea applies for people learning on their own: Pick one or two subjects to work on at a time, and pay careful attention to really figure them out.

Ask your own questions

While solving pre-defined problems and exercises is very useful, it can get monotonous. There's also something a bit passive about it. It's better than merely reading, but we're still leaving it up to someone else to test our knowledge.

---

[13]https://dev.to/t/explainlikeimfive

How about coming up with our own problems? When you're learning something new, ask yourself questions about it. What does this imply? Is there a more general way of looking at it? Is it similar to something else? Can it be applied like so?

With programming, you can write small programs to test your ideas. I highly recommend creating a coding playground folder. Any time you are trying to understand something, create a small example program to test it out in your playground. You can also come up with larger projects to work on. Such larger projects will force you out of the tidy confines of well-defined exercises. You'll need to integrate disparate areas of knowledge and think creatively to make your way around roadblocks.

Often questions will arise naturally when you're learning something new. It's easy to let those questions drift by and to forget about them. Or, a question may occur to you, but you'll dismiss it with negative self-talk, "oh that's a dumb question." That's really a disservice to yourself though. Being curious and making connections is a good thing. Censoring yourself, on the other hand, will just slow down your learning process.

> There are naive questions, tedious questions, ill-phrased questions, questions put after inadequate self-criticism. But every question is a cry to understand the world. There is no such thing as a dumb question.
>
> ~ *Carl Sagan*

You may find it helpful to have a notebook (or note app on your phone) always nearby. As soon as a question comes up, make a note of it. Then see if you can figure out the answer yourself. If so, great. If not, that's okay too. It's still good that you thought of your own brand new question! Now you can practice your research skills to get an answer.

As an example, a while ago I was writing some JavaScript code using async functions. As I was working, it occurred to me that it would be nice to combine a generator function and an async function together. I didn't know whether that was possible. After doing a bit of research, I found out that asynchronous iterators and generators had been proposed as a new feature for JavaScript. As of 2019, the new syntax is part of the ECMAScript 2020 Language Specification. It's also already supported by Node.js and by several major browsers.

When you take a hands-on approach to learning, I think you'll find that questions will naturally come up. If you want to practice though, try thinking about ways that an existing concept can be extended or combined with something else. Asking yourself questions is like exercising a muscle. The more you practice, the easier it will get.

Challenge your material

Whenever you're learning something, challenge the material and look for mistakes. Don't just take everything as gospel. Even when there aren't mistakes, this kind of active learning will ensure that you really do get it. When you challenge the material, it makes you explore edge cases and counter-intuitive possibilities. Doing so will make your understanding robust. You'll know how something works, and you'll also know in a hands-on, concrete way, the limitations and exceptions that go along with it.

A friend of mine told me a story from when she was in high school. She was learning special relativity in physics, and kept pestering her teacher with examples that seemed to defy the principles of relativity. I think her teacher was not equipped to answer those questions properly. It's actually well-known that there are a lot of scenarios in special relativity that initially seem to violate the rules. Understanding those edge cases is essential to have a proper understanding of the subject. I think what my friend was doing was great, and it's too bad that her teacher didn't understand the material well enough to encourage her properly.

Go back and review

Sometimes we don't realize that we missed something in our study until later. We start a new topic and suddenly things we thought we understood become confusing. That's a good time to stop and go back to review that earlier subject matter. Don't just re-read it passively though. Go hunting for insights relative to the new information you're grappling with. *Real understanding is not a linear process. It's iterative.* There is a continual need to go back and shore up gaps in our learning that maybe we didn't know were there, or that reappear over time as we forget things.

When I am studying something new myself, I find that I will regularly return to the same material several times. The first time I may struggle with completely new concepts. The next time around, I will start to get it. The third time, I begin to focus in on a smaller number of things that stand out as being harder than the rest. As time goes on I come up with more of my own questions and sometimes push the material in directions that are not mentioned in the book, article, or tutorial that I've been reading.

It can also be okay to study something up to a point, put it away, and return to it later on. Often we can acquire background knowledge in the meantime that makes us more prepared to tackle the material again once we come back to it.

Fundamentals are important

Often, especially in the field of technology, there tends to be a bit of an obsession with specifics, like a particular programming language, library, or framework. I think this is a tendency we should resist, especially since technologies go through such incredible turnover. The darling of the moment may be all but forgotten in a couple of years.

If you start your education with overly specific technologies, I believe it will limit your ability to adapt, or to switch from one area to another. In addition, when we learn a particular technology in isolation, it often makes our level of understanding more superficial. It means that as soon as we leave the comfort zone of the context in which we learned the technology, we can quickly become lost.

Focussing on fundamentals means trying to identify the core concepts and building blocks under-lying any technology or paradigm. Doing so is like having a good understanding of how to build things using lego blocks. It gives you the power to imagine any structure and build that from scratch rather than having to follow the blueprint that comes with a pre-packaged set.

Here's one possible example: Let's say you've learned how to use several frameworks and libraries for a front-end application. Perhaps you've used a CSS library like Bootstrap or a JavaScript framework like React, Vue, or Angular. *Do you know what problems these frameworks are trying to solve?* It can be helpful to develop a small browser application using only HTML, CSS, and plain Javascript—no CSS framework, no JavaScript framework, nothing else. You'd be responsible for updating the page yourself whenever something changes. You'd also be responsible for making sure your JavaScript works properly for every browser that you want to support. Doing something like this can provide insight into why we use certain technologies. It also tends to make it easier to learn a new technology in the same general category, because you understand the underlying motivation of its developers.

More generally, it's always good to delve into the basics of computer science. You can consider investing some time learning about boolean logic, electronics, data structures, algorithms, operating systems, networking protocols, databases, computer graphics, AI and machine learning, bioinformatics and genomics, discrete math, linear and abstract algebra, probability and statistics, calculus, etc. There are so many fascinating fields that computer programming touches or relies on. Building up the depth of your knowledge in such fundamental areas will enrich your understanding and appreciation. Don't worry about trying to do this all at once though! (Unless you're doing a C.S. degree, that is.) If you can pick one or two areas at a time, and just build up your knowledge gradually, that's great. Over time, every small step will add up.

Any specific technology can be seen as some combination of fundamental ideas applied in a particular way. Looking at things in this way is very powerful. It's like a superpower, allowing you to pick up new things quickly and leaving your colleagues wondering how you did it!

How to code (in one chapter)

Isaac Lyman

Note: This is the longest chapter by far. It also contains a fair amount of sarcasm. Many people appreciate the light humor in such a long read, but be sure to take it with a grain of salt.

```
1   (function () {
2     01001001 00100000
3     01100001 01101101
4     00100000 01110011
5     01110101 01100011
6     01101000 00100000
7     01100001 00100000
8     01101100 01100101
9     01100101 01110100
10    00100000 01100011
11    01101111 01100100
12    01100101 01110010
13  })();
```

This chapter is not a complete coding manual. It's a drive-through introduction to *just enough* coding concepts and keywords to get you from zero to a basic script.

First of all: take a deep breath. The picture above isn't real code. At least, it isn't code that anyone uses. Real code—what I write on the job—is mostly composed of English words, symbols, numbers (all ten of 'em, not just ones and zeros), and made-up names. Once you learn a bit of vocabulary, it's readable. I'm going to cover each of these later on.

Let's get started.

What is a computer program?

A computer program—also known as an *app*, an *application*, or a piece of *software*—is a collection of many lines of special text. They're special because a computer can understand them, and computers are incredibly dumb. The smallest practical apps have a hundred or so lines of text in them. The largest apps have billions[14].

---

[14]http://cacm.acm.org/magazines/2016/7/204032-why-google-stores-billions-of-lines-of-code-in-a-single-repository/fulltext

We call this special text *code*. Code is a set of step-by-step instructions, like a recipe. It tells computers what to do with *data*. Data is any piece of information that a computer can hold in its memory. Modern computers are pretty good at holding things like dates and sentences. If you have a Twitter account, then Twitter's got some flat, ugly computers at a warehouse that are holding your birthday and every tweet you've ever tweeted. Along with 300 million other people's birthdays and tweets.

Source: https://commons.wikimedia.org/wiki/File:CERN_Server_03.jpg[15]. Unmodified image licensed under CC BY-SA 3.0[16] by Florian Hirzinger

That's all data. Don't worry, the computers aren't sitting around reading your old tweets for fun. And if they did, it wouldn't be "fun," anyway. It would be painful. Your tweets are dumb, just like mine.

When you visit twitter.com, your computer borrows a whole bunch of code from one of those ugly warehouse computers. It speed-reads the heck out of that code. And then it *executes* that code, which means that the computer does exactly what the step-by-step instructions tell it to do.

If the instructions are written very carefully, it's all peaches from here on out. Twitter will work. It will publish your dumb tweets to the entire world. It will let you read other people's dumb tweets. It will let you "like" those tweets.

If there is any flaw in those instructions—anything from a typo to complete misinterpretation of the data—then Twitter will not work. It will show an "Error" message, or crash the app, or suffer in silence, secretly doing things with your data that you would prefer it not to.

That's the catch. Coding isn't very hard. It requires you to memorize a couple hundred terms and learn some grammar rules—you could do this with English (or your native language) by the time you were two, and human languages are a *mess*. What *is* hard is being called out by an anal-retentive computer every time you press a wrong key or misunderstand a concept. The hard part about coding is the sheer amount of frustration you have to absorb.

The fun part is the problem-solving. In modern software, real-world problems become puzzles that can be solved by code—but only after you truly understand them. Once you wrap your mind around every possible permutation of a problem, you can write code that addresses it thoroughly, step by step.

The tools of the trade

A programmer's toolbox typically consists of a few things:

- A computer.
- An internet connection. You need an internet connection so you can use Google. When you don't know how to do something (which happens about 787283493857 times per day) you Google it. When your app gives you an error message, you Google it. You Google everything.
- A code editor (or an IDE, which is a code editor on steroids). Think of it as Microsoft Word for coding. It helps you organize and proofread your code.
- A compiler or interpreter. This is a program that reads your code, tries to find mistakes so it can bug you about them, gathers your code into a nice little package, and then passes it on to the computer to execute. It does a lot of other things, too, but these are the things you need to know about right now.
- A good pair of headphones. These help you ignore people so you can focus.

You probably already have a computer. Since you downloaded this book, you definitely have an internet connection and an interpreter (Firefox and Chrome have interpreters built in). There are plenty of free code editors available online (like VS Code[17] or Atom[18]). I can't help you with the headphones, but a good alternative is staring at people until they leave.

So you're all set, right?

Programming languages

There are thousands of programming languages in the world. Many of them are dumb[19] and useless[20]. You can have a long and happy career only knowing three or four—but don't worry, this isn't as hard as learning three or four human languages.

Programming languages are often described by their *paradigm*, which is a way of categorizing the kinds of features they have. For example, JavaScript is the language that all web browsers run, and

---

[17]https://code.visualstudio.com/

[18]https://atom.io/

[19]https://en.wikipedia.org/wiki/Esoteric_programming_language

[20]https://en.wikipedia.org/wiki/Code_golf#Dedicated_golfing_languages

possibly the most popular programming language in the world. It has a diverse feature set; I might say that JavaScript supports imperative, structured, object-oriented, and event-driven paradigms. And you might say I'm a pretentious geek.

You don't need to know what all those words mean. What you do need to know is that programming languages with similar paradigms usually have similar *syntax*—that is, vocabulary and grammar. So once you've learned one language (like JavaScript), you're already 75% of the way to learning similar languages, like Python and Ruby.

The best coders understand problems in terms of an *algorithm*—a series of steps that can be used to do a certain thing, even if the details are different each time. Have you ever bought something on Amazon? The checkout experience is a sort of algorithm. No matter what you're buying, the steps are roughly the same: fill up your cart, choose your credit card and shipping address, pick a shipping speed and place your order. The code, in fact, is the same for each purchase. The difference is all in the data. Now get this: every algorithm that can possibly exist can be written in every normal programming language. It's a mathematical fact[21]. Once you learn to think in algorithms, the programming language is secondary. Sure, it kicks and drags its feet a little. But in the end it's not about the keywords and symbols you're using. It's about the processes you're describing.

From here on out, I'm going to use the JavaScript programming language to give examples. I'm doing this for my benefit, not yours. I'm good at JavaScript.

Code examples will be printed in monospace[22], which is a special typeface that `looks like this`. Monospaced fonts give the same exact width to every letter, number, symbol and space. All code is written in monospace even though it is harder to read than normal fonts. This is because it helps align blocks of code and allows coders to give equal attention to every letter and symbol, which helps them avoid errors. As an example, look at the following sentence in both a regular font and monospace:

Bob went out for the weekend and borrowed Alice''s horse wihout asking.

```
Bob went out for   the weekend and borrowed Alice''s horse wihout asking.
```

There are three mistakes in the sentence: the extra space after "for", the extra apostrophe in "Alice's", and Bob's exploitation of Alice's friendship and trust. Oh, and "without" is misspelled. You probably saw all these mistakes in the first sentence, but they're more obvious in the second one, and *obvious* is your best friend when you're scanning a 200-line code document.

Whenever you read something written in monospace, it's okay if you do a robot voice in your head.

---

[21]https://en.wikipedia.org/wiki/Turing_completeness
[22]https://en.wikipedia.org/wiki/Monospaced_font

Putting data in code

Enough background: let's write some code. The most basic building block of a computer program is a *variable*. A variable is a name for a piece of data, like a number or a sentence. You have to name your data.

There are two reasons you name your data:

1. You don't know what it is beforehand. Does Facebook know your birthday before you type it in? No, of course not. Facebook's code is using a name like `humans_birthday` behind the scenes (the underscore is there because variable names can't have spaces in them). It attaches that name to whatever birthday you type in. That way, the code can be exactly the same whether your birthday is June 10th, September 9th, or December 86th. It just moves `humans_birthday` around in the program until it reaches an ugly warehouse computer.

2. You don't want to forget what it means. Suppose the computer program needs to know that December 86th isn't a real date. So somewhere you have to tell it that December has 31 days. 31 is a number, a piece of data. But if you're using the number 31 all over your code, and also using numbers like 30 and 28 (because, thank goodness, December isn't the only month), your code is going to be confusing to read. What are all those numbers for? So you name them. 31 becomes `the_number_of_days_in_december`, and your code becomes self-explanatory. Beautiful.

Computers expect you to *declare* your variables. A variable declaration is like a birth certificate for a piece of data. It looks like this:

```
1   var the_number_of_days_in_december
```

The operative word here is `var`. It's short for "variable." The abbreviation is nice because it's faster to type. It can also be typed with only one hand, so if all you're doing is declaring variables all day, your other hand is free to do awesome things like juice grapefruits and practice with a quarterstaff.

Another thing you do with variables is *assign* them. This is where you attach the name to a piece of data. It looks like this:

```
1   the_number_of_days_in_december = 31
```

Easy stuff. You declare the variable, then you assign it, and then any time you want to use the number 31 in your program, you can type `the_number_of_days_in_december` and the computer will know what you mean.

You don't have to assign every variable to an explicit piece of data when you write your program. You can declare variables and assign them to things that don't exist yet. For example, you can declare `var humans_birthday` and tell the app to wait for the user to type it in. Whatever they type will become `humans_birthday`. You don't even have to worry about it.

Variables can hold way more than just numbers and dates. For example, you can declare a *string*, or a piece of text:

```
1   var great_song_lyrics = 'La la la, la la la tonight'
```

Whoa. Curveball. I just declared a variable and assigned it *at the same time*. I'm so hecking efficient. Bring this man a grapefruit.

Now I can write `great_song_lyrics` in my code, wherever I want, and the computer will know that I mean `'La la la, la la la tonight'`. It's like we're talking...in *code*.

Don't believe me? Try it right now. If you're reading this on your phone, you'll need to open a web browser, like Chrome or Firefox, on a computer. Press the F12 key on your keyboard (if you're using Safari, you'll have to find the developer tools in the menus). You'll see something like this:

This may be aligned to the right or bottom edge of your browser.

Make sure the "Console" tab is selected. Click in the blank area next to the › symbol, type a variable declaration and assignment, and press Enter:

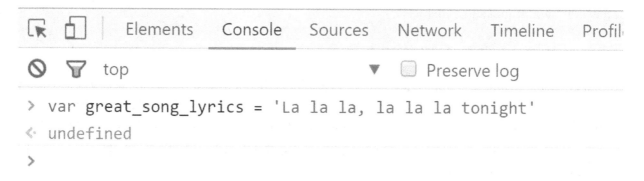

The console is saying `undefined` because the line of code you typed didn't produce any data. That's okay, it wasn't supposed to. Now type the name of your variable and press Enter again:

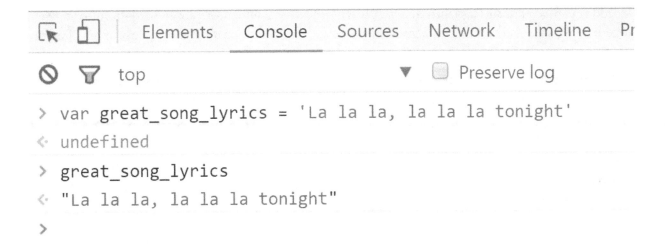

Hooray! The console (which is an *interpreter*) understands your variable. The variable great_song_-lyrics *evaluated* (it was understood) as "La la la, la la la tonight". That's perfect (by the way, it doesn't matter if you use single quotes ' or double quotes " as long as you use them in matching pairs).

We'll talk about other things variables can hold in just a second.

Many programming languages require you to be specific about what *kind* of variable you're declaring. In C++, for example, there is no var keyword. There's an int keyword (for declaring small whole numbers), a long keyword (for declaring big whole numbers), float and double keywords (for declaring decimal numbers), a string keyword (for declaring pieces of text), and a few others. Don't worry about that right now. You can learn it later.

Complex types

Objects

An important part of coding is learning how to organize data. Take the birthday example: Facebook has hundreds of millions of birthdays (and anniversaries and breakup dates) stored in computer memory in its warehouse. How does it know what's what? If I gave you a list of a billion dates, would you know who they belong to and what they're for? Of course you would, because you are the great Calendifus, Greek god of randomly significant dates.

Luckily, Facebook doesn't just have a pile of arbitrary dates sitting around. They connect your birthday, your anniversary, your hometown, your employment history, your name, and everything else they know about you together with a unique ID (like the one on your Social Security card or your driver's license). It's probably a big number that they picked out of a hat, so to speak. That is, you are number 12884002, and every piece of data they have on you has a label that says "12884002", and when you log in they look up everything with that number on it. It's all organized just like that.

In code, you would do this with an *object*. An object is a bunch of pieces of data all organized together. We can also call this an *associative array*, a *dictionary*, or a *map*. But most often I just say *object*.

In JavaScript, objects are declared and assigned much like other variables. Here's an example object:

```
1   var human = {
2     id: 12884002,
3     age: 28,
4     name: 'Bob',
5     favorite_song: 'Half Light, by Athlete'
6   }
```

Each piece of data in an object is like a seesaw. The name is on the left, the data is on the right, and there's a : in the middle to balance on. Really all we've done is declare four variables: the first two are numbers, and the last two are strings. But they're organized together so we can find them whenever we need to know something about human. And instead of calling them "variables," we call them "properties" or "fields." An object can have any properties you want, as long as you put them all together inside of { curly brackets }.

We can move the human object around and refer to it just like any other variable. The computer knows what we mean. If we ever want to refer to just one property of human, we use a dot, like this:

```
1   human.id
2   human.age
3   human.name
4   human.favorite_song
```

Each of these is just like any other variable. We can assign something to it and refer to it later. Want to change Bob's name? Easy:

```
human.name = 'Alice'
```

And that's that. It's a really good upgrade, isn't it? From now on, whenever you type human.name, it will refer to "Alice".

Arrays

Sometimes you don't want to think up a unique name for every property in an object, especially if they're all very similar. Or you don't know how many there are going to be. That's when it's time to use an *array*, which is a list of similar pieces of data. Arrays can grow or shrink as needed.

A good example is all your dumb tweets. Twitter doesn't know how many tweets you're going to write. You started at 0, and look where you are now. Twitter could use an array to hold them all. Arrays in JavaScript look like this:

```
1  var dumb_tweets = [
2    'Hello, Twitter!',
3    'My friends are so cool',
4    'Does anyone want a LaCroix?'
5  ]
```

Remember how objects used { curly brackets } ? Arrays use [square brackets]. This array has three strings in it, separated by commas. And yes, it's a variable just like anything else. You can use dumb_tweets anywhere in your code, and it will refer to the array we defined just now.

If you want to refer to a specific string in the array, you'd do it like this:

```
1  dumb_tweets[0]
2  dumb_tweets[1]
3  dumb_tweets[2]
```

We use the name of the array, dumb_tweets, and then inside of [square brackets] we use the number (or *index*) of the thing (or *element*) we want to refer to. I know it's weird that the first element in the array is number 0. But this is your life now. From this day forward, you will always begin counting at 0. It's the programmer way.

Each of the above expressions (an *expression* is any code that turns into a piece of data when you run it) is a variable. You can assign something new to it, if you want.

```
1  dumb_tweets[2] = 'I regret literally everything I have ever said'
```

Whatever happened to 'Does anyone want a LaCroix?'? It's gone forever. Swallowed by the abyss. G'bye!

Arrays can hold strings, numbers, dates, objects, and even other arrays. You can put arrays inside of arrays inside of arrays inside of arrays.

Photo: Lachlan Fearnley[23]. Unmodified image licensed under CC BY-SA 3.0[24]

Any time code or data gets all Russian-doll-ish like that, we say it's *nested*.

Arrays can also be properties of objects. An object can have a property that is an array of objects, each of which has a property that is an array of objects...and I've done it again. It sounds like a tax form, but it's how data is structured. For example, your Twitter account could be an object that has a property which is an array of tweets; each tweet could be an object that has properties that are arrays of replies, likes, and retweets; each reply, like or retweet could be an object that has properties that are the name, profile picture and bio of the user that gave them; and so on.

```
1   var nested_object = {
2     an_array: [
3       {
4         another_array: [
5           {
6             yet_another: [
7               {
8                 message: 'Blink twice if you need help'
9               }
10            ]
11          }
12        ]
13      }
```

---

[23]https://commons.wikimedia.org/wiki/File:Russian_Dolls.jpg
[24]https://creativecommons.org/licenses/by-sa/3.0/deed.en

```
14    ]
15  }
```

To access message, you can write:

```
1  nested_object.an_array[0].another_array[0].yet_another[0].message
```

And the computer will know that you mean 'Blink twice if you need help.'

Objects (continued)

One more trippy part, and then we can move on to the fun stuff.

Everything in JavaScript is secretly an object (don't tell! Its parents would be so mad). For example, our dumb_tweets array has a property that we never declared:

```
1  dumb_tweets.length
```

What the heck is length? Well, it's a property that JavaScript creates and updates for you automatically. It tells you how many elements are in the array. In this case it would be 3. There are 3 elements in the array. Go count 'em, but don't start from 0 this time because I lied and you're only supposed to start counting from 0 on special occasions. Dang it.

APIs

Time for a scary campfire story.

Once upon a time, in an alternate universe, there was a programmer named McChuck. He was the only coder in the whole universe. He had to write all the code that would ever exist, all by himself.

Photo: hannah k[25]. Unmodified image licensed under CC BY 2.0[26]

Sheesh, it was just a story. Calm down.

The truth is that no coder is an island. Nobody starts from scratch. We're all constantly using code we didn't write—buckets of it, in fact.

Even if you are a prolific coder and write millions of lines of code in your lifetime, you will use far more lines of code that someone else wrote. Most of this code will come from complete strangers. Some of those strangers will be dead. Their code lives on, even though the fingers that typed it are decomposing in a grave. It's zombie code. But instead of eating your brain, it saves your brain from doing a lot of hard work. Best. zombie. ever.

How do you use this zombie code? Copy and paste? Occasionally, yes, but not often. Most of the time you'll access it through an Application Programming Interface or *API*. An API is a bundled-up set of properties and *methods* (purpose-built pieces of code) that are named, like variables, so you can refer to them by their name and let them do their thing. They do all kinds of useful things for you.

JavaScript arrays have their own API. The `length` property is part of this API. Another part of it is the `push` method, which adds an element to the end of the array:

---

[25]https://www.flickr.com/photos/90692443@N05/8239219385

[26]https://creativecommons.org/licenses/by/2.0/

```
1   dumb_tweets.push('Man I hate good attitudes')
```

A method is like a property because you access it with a dot. A method is different from a property because you have to put (parentheses) after it. These parentheses are holding the data we want to add to our array. Now `dumb_tweets` has four elements. It looks like this:

```
1   [
2     "Hello, Twitter!",
3     "My friends are so cool",
4     "I regret literally everything I have ever said",
5     "Man I hate good attitudes"
6   ]
```

Remember, the index of this last element is 3 (because you started counting at 0). So you would refer to it as `dumb_tweets[3]`. And `dumb_tweets.length` would now evaluate to 4.

The JavaScript array API has a lot of different methods in it, but it's outside the purpose of this chapter to explain them all. You can see them in their full glory at this link[27].

Web browsers have a huge API that JavaScript coders use every day. This API has methods for things like animating stuff in a website, getting user input, communicating with other computers over the internet, manipulating strings, and loads of other stuff. Building a working vocabulary in this API is an essential part of becoming a web developer.

Functions

Function is another word for *method*. It's just a piece of code that does something and (usually) has a name. Functions are easy to declare in JavaScript:

```
1   function giveMeOne() {
2     return 1
3   }
```

We start with the keyword `function`. Then we give the function a name, just like if we were declaring a variable (here I've used capitalization, instead of underscores, to separate words). Then we use parentheses (you'll see why in a second). Then we use { curly brackets }. Inside the curly brackets are all the lines of code we want to execute whenever the function is *called* (whenever an expression refers to it by name).

The word `return` is another special keyword. It makes a *value* (a piece of data) pop out of the function. Then it ends the function (if you write any code after a `return` statement, that code won't execute). So you could do something like this:

---

[27]https://developer.mozilla.org/en-US/docs/Web/JavaScript/Reference/Global_Objects/Array

```
1   var the_loneliest_number = giveMeOne()
```

This isn't too hard, right? We declare a variable named `the_loneliest_number`. The assignment part of our statement calls `giveMeOne()`, and since that function says `return 1`, a 1 pops out. So our variable will hold the number 1. Go ahead and execute both of these blocks of code in your browser's console. Then type `the_loneliest_number`, press Enter, and you'll see that it evaluates to 1.

A function can be a property of an object. It can be an element of an array. It can return a number, a date, a string, an object, an array, another function, an array full of functions, and so forth. This stuff is like LEGO bricks. Put any kind of piece anywhere you want and it will fit.

`giveMeOne()` is kind of like `dumb_tweets.push()`. The main differences are:

1. `giveMeOne()` is a function we wrote by ourselves. `push()` is a function that some strangers wrote. It's okay, they don't mind if we use it.
2. `push()` is a method of `dumb_tweets` (and any other array we'll ever create). `giveMeOne()` is *global*, meaning that we don't need to refer to a specific object in order to use it.

You'll notice one more thing that seems different about them: `giveMeOne()` uses empty parentheses, but `push()` expects us to put a piece of data in the parentheses. In fact, `push()` would be useless if we couldn't tell it what to add to our array. The piece of data we give it is called an *argument*. An argument is just a piece of data that we drop into a function. Declaring a function that expects arguments looks like this:

```
1   function addTheseNumbersTogetherPlz(number1, number2) {
2       return number1 + number2
3   }
```

This function isn't too different from `giveMeOne()`. But instead of empty parentheses, these have variable names in them, separated by a comma. These are our arguments. The `return` statement does exactly what it looks like it's doing: it adds number1 and number2 together, then pops out the result. You'd call the function like this: `addTheseNumbersTogetherPlz(3, 4)`. And it would pop out a 7.

Ooh! Math! Scary, right? Almost all coding languages let you write math expressions the same way you used to write them in those bricky TI calculators you might have used in high school. You can use + to add, - to subtract, / to divide, * to multiply, (parentheses) to enforce an order of operations, % to get the remainder of division, and ^ to instantly grow a neckbeard (no, it doesn't do exponents; you need an API for that).

You could also write the function this way:

```
1  function addTheseNumbersTogetherPlz(number1, number2) {
2    var sum = number1 + number2
3
4    return sum
5  }
```

This function does *exactly the same thing*. It just uses a variable named sum as a middleman, where the result is stored so we can return it later.

There are many ways to write a function. You should choose the way that most clearly expresses what the code is doing. Code that is concise and easy to understand is often called *expressive* or *elegant*. There's an artistic pleasure in writing this kind of code.

> Programs must be written for people to read, and only incidentally for machines to execute.
>
> ~ *Harold Abelson*

Logical branches and comparisons

This is where code gets *extra* fun. (It was fun already.)

Computer programs don't do the same exact thing every time you run them. If they did, then video games would play themselves. That would be a letdown. You'd have to just sit there and watch the story play out on the screen, like a...I don't know, but it would be boring. There definitely wouldn't be an entire industry[28] dedicated to it.

Programs have to respond to different situations. They have to make decisions. And that's where things like if statements come in.

Let's say we're writing an app that determines whether a particular person is allowed to enter a nightclub. Pretend there's a method in the JavaScript API that gets a user's age. We'll call it getUserAge(). We'll also imagine that there are two other methods, allowThemInTheNightclub() and throwThemOutOnTheirButt(). How can we help our program decide which of these last two methods to call, based on the returned value of the first method?

---

[28]https://en.wikipedia.org/wiki/Film_industry

```
1   var age = getUserAge()
2
3   if (age >= 21) {
4     allowThemInTheNightclub()
5   } else {
6     throwThemOutOnTheirButt()
7   }
```

See how nice the alignment is on the right side? Monospace is great.

You already know what the first line does. age will hold a value like 13 or 21 or 101. Now we need to know: is age 21 or over? If so, they can party away. If not, they'll need to leave.

We do that using an if statement. if is a keyword that looks a little bit like a method. The argument it expects is an expression of some kind, usually a *comparison*. Comparisons take two values and compare them to each other, resulting in a value of true (if the comparison is true) or false (if it's not true). These two values are called *booleans* and they're the only two booleans in existence. Lucky they've got each other. We can make six different kinds of comparisons:

- === (three equals signs) compares the values on either side to see if they are exactly equal. If they are equal, the result is true. 6 === 6 would be true.
- !== compares the values on either side to see if they are *not* exactly equal. If they are *not* equal, the result is true. 6 !== 3 would be true.
- > checks to see if the value on the left side is bigger than the value on the right side. 6 > 3 would be true.
- < checks to see if the value on the *right* side is bigger than the value on the *left* side. 3 < 6 would be true.
- >= checks to see if the value on the left side is bigger than, or equal to, the value on the right side. 6 >= 6 and 6 >= 5 are both true.
- <= checks to see if the value on the *right* side is bigger than, or equal to, the value on the *left* side. 6 <= 6 and 6 <= 7 are both true.

if statements evaluate the comparison you give them. If it evaluates to true, they execute the code inside their *block* (the lines of code inside { curly brackets }). If it evaluates to false, they skip that code.

if statements can also have an else statement attached to their tail end. The else statement has a block that will be executed if the comparison is false. Look back at our nightclub app. It should make a lot of sense to you now.

Hey, we just made a bouncer *redundant* (he was replaced by a computer program). Isn't that a good feeling?

Loops

Sometimes, especially when you're working with an array, you want to execute a block of code several times in a row. This is *not* the time to use copy and paste. Instead, you should use a loop. The simplest kind of loop in JavaScript is a `while` loop:

```
1  var knock_knock_joke = ['Knock knock', "Who's there?", 'Banana', 'Banana who?']
2
3  var index = 0
4
5  while (index < knock_knock_joke.length) {
6    say(knock_knock_joke[index])
7
8    index = index + 1
9  }
```

`while` loops use the same syntax as `if` statements. You use parentheses, you pass in a comparison, you follow it up with a block. But an `if` block only executes the code inside of it once (or zero times, if the comparison evaluates to `false`). A `while` block executes the code inside of it *over and over again* until the condition is `false`. That is, it evaluates the condition; if it's `true`, it executes the block; then it evaluates the condition again; if `true`, it executes the block *again*; then it evaluates the condition again; and so on, forever. I've invented an imaginary API here that has a `say()` method, but everything else is regular JavaScript.

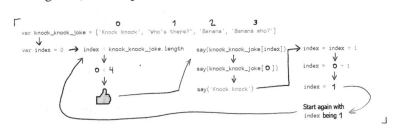

How many times will the loop execute? Well, the first time it evaluates the comparison, it checks to see if `index` (which is 0) is smaller than `knock_knock_joke.length` (which is—go on, count them—4). Since the comparison is `true`, it executes the code, which raps `knock_knock_joke[0]`, because `index` is still 0. Then the magic happens: it changes `index` to `index + 1`, or 0 + 1, which is 1. Then it evaluates the comparison expression again. 1 is still less than 4, so it executes the block again—but this time, since index is 1, it raps `knock_knock_joke[1]`. Get it? It will stop executing the block when `index` equals 4, which is good because `knock_knock_joke[4]` *doesn't exist*. When a loop operates on multiple elements in an array, we say it's *iterating*.

Null and undefined

If you declare a variable and do not assign a value to it, it will hold a special value called `undefined`. This is a geeky word that means "move along, nothing to see here." It's mostly useless.

JavaScript also has a special value called `null`. It means roughly the same thing as `undefined`. They really shouldn't have included both words in the language. But they did and it's too late now.

Scopes

Functions are very selfish. If you declare a variable inside of a function, the function won't let any of the code outside of itself use the variable. For example:

```
 1  function whatHappensInVegas() {
 2    var wildIndiscretions = ['partied', 'danced']
 3
 4    return 'I admit nothing'
 5  }
 6
 7  whatHappensInVegas()
 8  whatHappensInVegas()
 9  whatHappensInVegas()
10
11  if (wildIndiscretions.length > 0) {
12    getInTrouble()
13  }
```

We have a very simple function. It declares the variable `wildIndiscretions`, but it doesn't return it. The outside world knows nothing about it! We even run the function three times, because we're young and full of stamina. The `if` statement is trying to pry into the function's personal life, but it can't. The code inside of the `if` block will never execute. In fact, the comparison `wildIndiscretions.length > 0` will *throw an error* (it won't work and you'll see a message explaining why) because `wildIndiscretions` is `undefined` outside of the function `whatHappensInVegas`. It doesn't have *any* properties, let alone `length`.

However, if you move that `if` block inside the `function` block (before the `return` statement, of course) then it will gain access to `wildIndiscretions`. Hope you have a good lawyer!

Comments

It isn't always obvious what a piece of code is doing, or what still needs to be done with it. If you need to break out of the computer language and have some real talk about what's going on in the code (or just drop some dope lyrics), you can use a *comment*, or a line of code that the computer will ignore. You start a comment with `//` two forward slashes. Like this:

```
1   function isEven(num) {
2     // This function determines if "num" is even or odd.
3     //  If even, it returns true. If odd, it returns false.
4     // TO DO: add a second argument that lets you specify
5     //  a message to display if "num" is odd.
6
7     return num % 2 === 0
8
9     // Hey, yo, do it like Isaac
10    // If you ain't with me, baby ain't wise-aac
11  }
```

Don't worry about the maths in the `return` statement. I'm just demonstrating that you can use comments to explain what's going on, to leave a note for your future self, *and* to spit bars. The last usage is probably frowned upon in serious codebases. But don't let that hold you back. You were born to do what you were born to do.

Searching for clues

The last and most important thing I can teach you is this: when you don't know how to do something, immediately go to google.com and ask. The generosity of the programming community will astound you. Thousands of developers all around the world have freely shared their code and knowledge on sites like GitHub[29] and Stack Overflow[30], which means that all you need to become an expert in any programming language is a steady internet connection and the ability to read.

Good Google queries take a little bit of practice to write. A good template is something like this:

```
[programming language] how to [something]
```

For example, want to know how to remove an element from an array in JavaScript? I'm not gonna teach you. Try typing this into Google: "JavaScript how to remove an element from an array". The first few results should give you all the information you need (with examples).

For more discussion of this topic, see Yechiel's chapter "Learning to learn".

What is an application?

Most large-scale apps use all the concepts and keywords I've described. Their code comprises thousands upon thousands of lines of code, all built from these same basic elements. So what are they *doing*?

On a basic level, they're receiving *inputs* (data that enters the code from somewhere else, like a user's keyboard), transforming them (often by iterating over them, doing maths on them, or reorganizing

---

[29]https://github.com/
[30]http://stackoverflow.com/

their properties), and providing *outputs* (data that leaves the code). Every computer program can be described in terms of its inputs and outputs. Every programming language has methods in its API for accepting inputs and providing outputs.

An ice maker is a good analogy for a computer program. Its inputs are water and electricity (they come from an API known as "municipal utilities"). Its output is ice (which is submitted to an API known as "a tall glass of Coke"). Do you care what happens in the middle? Not right now, as long as you get your ice without too much trouble. But someday the ice maker will break down. And whoever has to fix it will care *a lot* about how simple, robust and well-built its internal components are.

A coder's job isn't just to provide the ice, although that's important. A coder's job is to make sure that when the ice maker breaks, the person who has to fix it doesn't develop an explosive headache in the process. That's the difference between an amateur coder and a pro.

Conclusion

You've done good. I've taught you enough programming basics that, with a little imagination and plenty of Googling, you can teach yourself everything you need to know to write apps. If you want to.

You may still feel like you're missing some vital information. And you are. But you'll never learn it all, and this is a good start.

If you're still shaky on your feet, go check out some more JavaScript tutorials. There are tons of free ones online on sites like Codecademy[31]. And once you feel confident enough to write some code of your own, *go build something.* There's no substitute for getting your hands dirty.

---

[31]https://www.codecademy.com/learn/introduction-to-javascript

Steps to better code

Isaac Lyman

When you start out coding, you usually spend a year or two completely oblivious to the rules of "good code." You may hear words like "elegant" or "clean" tossed around, but you can't define them. That's okay. For a programmer without any experience, the main metric worth keeping tabs on is "does it work?"

Soon, though, you'll need to raise your expectations. Good code doesn't just *work*. It's simple, modular, testable, maintainable, thoughtful. Some of these terms may apply to your code without you even knowing it, but probably not. If you're lucky, your team carefully plans and architects its code solutions and guides you gently, trusting that you'll develop an intuition for well-written software. If you're not lucky, they wince[32] or[33] complain[34] every time they see your code. Either way, you can get a lot of mileage out of learning a few universal principles.

Take, for example, the *global variable*: a variable that can be used anywhere in the project. Suppose your app has a `username` variable that's set when the user logs in and can be accessed from any function in the app just by referencing the variable name—that's a global variable. Global variables are universally despised by bloggers and style guides, but most entry-level coders don't understand why. The reason is—and pay attention, because this is the reason for almost all best practices in coding—that *it makes the code faster to write, but harder to understand.* In this case, a global variable makes it really easy to insert the user's username into the app anywhere you want, which may mean fewer lines of code and fewer minutes until you finish your current task. That's false comfort, though: you've sacrificed safety for convenience. If you discover a bug involving `username`, you will have to debug not just a single file or function, but the entire project. I'll talk more about this later.

The difference between "good code" and "bad code" isn't usually based on the way it affects *you* as you write it. Code is always a shared resource: you share it with other open-source contributors, or with the other developers on your team, or with the person who will have your job in the future, or with "future you" (who won't have a clue what "present you" was thinking), or even just with "debugging you," who is going through your fresh code looking for bugs and is totally frustrated. All of these people will be grateful if your code makes sense. It will make their job easier and less stressful. In this way, writing good code is a form of professional courtesy.

You may still be skeptical, but read on—I'll talk about several principles that lead to good code and try to justify each one.

---

[32] https://xkcd.com/1513/
[33] https://xkcd.com/1695/
[34] https://xkcd.com/1833/

0. Naming things

> There are only two hard things in Computer Science: cache invalidation and naming things.
>
> ~ Phil Karlton

Well-written code tells a story, and is often readable even for someone who only has a passing familiarity with code. An important part of this is well-named variables, classes, files, and methods. When naming something, it's far more important to be descriptive than brief: a variable name like "elementarySchoolStudentLastNameFirstLetterRegEx" may have room for improvement, but it's much better than "b". It's useful to be able to know what something is immediately, right when you look at it, even if you haven't read the rest of the file or project. And that goes double for public fields and methods. Any element of code whose name doesn't fully communicate its purpose is one more thing you have to think about every time you use or modify it.

Beyond descriptiveness, *uniqueness* is also valuable. Sometimes when modifying code, you'll want to do a project-wide search for a method or variable and find everywhere it's being used. In this situation it's best if its name is unique. If you've been calling things `method1` and `stringA`, your search results will be full of irrelevant stuff and it will be hard to make changes without breaking anything.

Renaming things is a great way to improve code quality as a junior developer. Make sure you know the naming conventions of your team and project—if they use underscores or capital letters to separate words, if they like to include a variable's type in its name, and so on—then find a couple of things with confusing names and suggest better ones.

1. Separation of concerns

A fair analogy for coding is writing a recipe. In simple recipes, each step depends on the one before it, and once all the steps are complete, the recipe is done. But if you've ever tried to follow a more complex recipe, you've probably experienced the stress of having two pots boiling on the stove, a plate spinning in the microwave, three kinds of vegetables half-chopped on a cutting board, and a smorgasbord of spice and herb shakers strewn across the countertop (and you can't remember which ones you've already added).

Having another cook in the kitchen complicates the problem as often as it simplifies it. You waste time coordinating, handing things back and forth, and fighting over stove space and oven temperature. It takes practice to figure out how to do it well.

If you know you're going to have several cooks in the kitchen, wouldn't it be more efficient for the recipe to be split into mostly-independent sub-recipes? Then you could hand part of the recipe to each cook and they could work with as little interaction as possible. One of them is boiling water for pasta. One of them is chopping and cooking vegetables. One of them is shredding cheese. One of them is making sauce. And the points of interaction are clearly defined, so each of them knows when to hand off their work.

The worst form of code is like a simple recipe: a bunch of steps in order, each written out in the same space, and listed from top to bottom. In order to understand it and modify it, you have to read the whole thing a couple of times. A variable on line 2 could affect an operation on line 832, and the only way to find out is to read the entire program.

A slightly better form of code is like having a second cook in the kitchen. You hand off some operations to other parts of the program, but your goal is mostly to make your files smaller, not necessarily to organize and simplify your code. It's an improvement, just not taken far enough.

The best form of code is like splitting a recipe into sub-recipes, usually called "modules" or "classes" in code. Each module is concerned with a single simple operation or piece of data. The vegetable chef shouldn't have to worry about the sauce ingredients, and the person cooking pasta shouldn't have to worry about the cheese grater. Their concerns are separated (hence the term *separation of concerns*).

The benefits to this are significant. Suppose a coder needs to modify the program later—to make it gluten-free for a client with celiac disease or to add a seasonal vegetable. That coder will only need to read, understand and modify one small part of the program. If all of the code dealing with vegetables is contained in a single small class with a few well-defined inputs and outputs, the coder never needs to worry that adding a vegetable will ruin the sauce.

The goal here is to make sure that, to make any given change, the coder has to think about as few parts of the program as possible, instead of all the parts at once.

2. Global variables (are bad)

Let's jump back to your username variable. When you built the login page for your app, you realized you'd need to display the user's username in a few other places, like perhaps the site header and the settings page. So you take the path of least resistance: you create it as a global variable. In Python, it's declared with the global keyword. In JavaScript, it's a property of the window object. It seems like a good solution. Anywhere you need to show the username, you just pop in the username variable and you're on your way. Why aren't all variables maintained like this?

Then things go sideways. There's a bug in the code, and it has something to do with username. Despite the availability of an instant search tool in most code editors, this is going to take a while to fix. You'll search username and there will be hundreds or thousands of results; some will be the global variable you set up at the beginning of the project, some will be other variables that also happen to be named username, and some will be the word "username" in a comment, class name, method name, and so forth. You can refine your search and reduce the amount of noise, but debugging will still take longer than it should.

The solution is to put username where it belongs: inside of a container (e.g. an object) that gets imported or passed as an argument to the classes and methods that need it. This container can also hold similar pieces of data—anything that's set at login is a good candidate (but don't store the password. Don't ever store a password without encryption). If you're so inclined, you can make this container immutable, so that once `username` is set, it can't ever be changed. This will make debugging extremely easy, even if `username` is used tens of thousands of times in your app.

Coding this way will make your life easier. You'll always be able to find the data you're looking for, in exactly one place. And if you ever need to track when a piece of data is used or changed, you can add some functionality to your object (like a *getter* and *setter*—see Appendix A) and be on your way.

3. DRY

Suppose you're building a website that sells fancy hats. You build a page for the first hat and write the code for adding it to someone's shopping cart. You've got 24 more hats, so you build pages for them, then copy the shopping cart code from the first page and paste it into each one. Everything is working great. You make little modifications here and there: some of the hats have optional feathers or lace, others have a lot of color options. After a while, that shopping cart code doesn't look quite the same on any two pages.

Then you learn there's a bug in the original shopping cart code and it's making your customers upset. You need to fix it right away. And you realize you've made a huge mistake: since you copied and pasted the code from one page to another, you have to fix it 25 times, once for each fancy hat. You have to do it by hand, since the code is a little different on each page. That's going to take forever. You're up late rubbing your eyes and coding fix after tedious fix, and your customers are buying their fancy hats from competitors.

Ugh.

There's a better way: next time you build a website, don't be so quick to copy and paste. Write the code for the first page, then if you need some of that code in other pages, put it in a class method or a function and let each page refer to it, passing in arguments to handle any little differences between them.

DRY stands for "Don't Repeat Yourself." It's a good guideline to remember.

The goal is this: if an operation needs to change in some way, you should only have to modify a single class or method. This is quicker and far more reliable than trying to maintain several copies of the same code.

Don't take it too far, though—if two operations are really different, let them be different. Trying to force two distinct pieces of code into the same function can result in strange and confusing code.

Many programmers prefer the acronym WET, for "Write Everything Twice." That is, go ahead and copy something once, but if you find yourself with three copies of the same code, then it's time to refactor them into shared functionality. This is a very practical way to apply the spirit of DRY without overdoing it.

4. Hiding complexity

Imagine I'm selling you a car. It will take some training for you to learn how to use it.

To start the car, take red wire #2 and white wire #7 and touch them together while kicking the engine-rev pinwheel with your foot and pouring an appropriate amount of fuel into the injector, which you'll find under the center console. Once the car has started, reach into the gearbox and push the layshaft into place against the first gear on the differential shaft. To accelerate, increase the flow of gasoline into the injector. To brake, hold your feet against the tires.

I'm sure this car frustrates you as much as it frustrates me. Now let's channel that angst toward code elements with over-complicated interfaces.

When you build a class or method, the first thing you write should be the *interface*: the part that a different piece of code (a caller) would need to know about in order to use the class or method. For a method, this is also called the *signature*. Every time you look up a function or class in API documentation (like on MDN Web Docs[35] or the Python documentation[36]), what you're seeing is the interface—only what you need to know to use it, without any of the code it contains.

An interface should be simple but expressive. It should make sense in plain English, without expecting the caller to know about the order in which things happen, data that the caller isn't responsible for, or external variables.

This is a bad interface:

```
1  function addTwoNumbersTogether(
2    number1, number2, memoizedResults, globalContext, sumElement, addFn
3  ) // returns an array
```

This is a good interface:

```
1  function addTwoNumbersTogether(
2    number1, number2
3  ) // returns a number
```

If an interface can be smaller, it should be. If a value you're providing with an argument could be calculated from other values instead, it probably shouldn't be an argument (or the others shouldn't be). If a method has more than a few parameters, you should ask yourself if you're doing something wrong (although you might make an exception for some class constructors).

Don't take this too far. If you're setting and using global variables in order to avoid passing arguments to a function, you're doing it wrong. If a method requires a lot of different pieces of data, try splitting it out into more specific functions; if that's not possible, create a class or object specifically for passing this data around.

Remember that *all methods and data* that are in a class but can be accessed from outside of that class are part of its interface. This means you should make as many methods and fields private as you possibly can. In JavaScript, variables declared using var, let, or const are automatically private

---

[35]https://developer.mozilla.org/en-US/
[36]https://docs.python.org/3/

to the function they're declared in, as long as you don't return them or assign them to an object; in many other languages, there is a `private` keyword. This should be your best friend. Only make data public on a need-to-know basis.

5. Proximity

Declare things as close as possible to where they're used.

Your instinctive urge to organize can work against you here. You may think an organized method looks like this:

```
1   function () {
2     var a = getA(),
3       b = getB(),
4       c = getC(),
5       d = getD();
6
7     doSomething(b);
8     doAnotherThing(a);
9     doOtherStuff(c);
10    finishUp(d);
11  }
```

`getA()` and its compatriots aren't defined in this snippet, but imagine that they return useful values.

In a small method like this, you may be forgiven for thinking the code is well-organized and easy to read. But it's not. d, for some reason, is declared on line 5 even though it isn't used until line 10, which means you have to read *almost the entire method* to make sure it isn't used anywhere else.

A better method looks like this:

```
1   function () {
2     var b = getB();
3     doSomething(b);
4
5     var a = getA();
6     doAnotherThing(a);
7
8     var c = getC();
9     doOtherStuff(c);
10
11    var d = getD();
12    finishUp(d);
13  }
```

Now it's clear when a variable is going to be used: immediately after it's declared.

Most of the time the situation isn't so simple; what if b needs to be passed to both doSomething() and doOtherStuff()? In that case, it's your job to weigh the options and make sure the method is still simple and readable (usually by keeping it short and using more descriptive variable names than a and b). In any case, make sure you don't declare b until immediately before its first use, and use it in the shortest possible code segment.

If you do this consistently, you'll sometimes find that part of a method is completely independent from the code above and beneath it. This is a good opportunity to extract it into its own method. Even if that method is only used once, it will be valuable as a way to enclose all the parts of an operation in an easily understandable, well-named block.

6. Deep nesting (is bad)

JavaScript is known for an uncomfortable situation known as "callback hell":

```
1  function getSumOfLetters(callback, errorCallback) {
2    getA().then(a => {
3      getB().then(b => {
4        getC().then(c => {
5          getD().then(d => {
6            getE().then(e => {
7              getF().then(f => {
8                postSum([a, b, c, d, e, f]).then(
9                  sum => callback(sum),
10                 err => errorCallback(err)
11               )
12             })
13           })
14         })
15       })
16     })
17   })
18 }
```

See that trail of }) running down the last several lines? That's the calling card of callback hell. It's avoidable, but that's a subject that plenty of other writers have already addressed.

What I want you to consider is something more like "if hell."

```
1   callApi(function(result) {
2     try {
3       if (result.status === 0) {
4         model.apiCall.success = true
5
6         if (result.data.items.length > 0) {
7           model.apiCall.numOfItems = result.data.items.length
8
9           if (isValid(result.data)) {
10            model.apiCall.result = result.data
11          }
12        }
13      }
14    } catch (e) {
15      // ignore errors
16    }
17  })
```

Count the pairs of { curly braces }. Six, five of which are nested. That's too many. This block of code is hard to read, partially because the code is about to creep off the right side of the screen and programmers hate horizontal scrolling, and partially because you have to read all the if conditions to figure out how you got to line 10.

try and catch are keywords you may not have encountered yet. Any time an error occurs inside of a try block, it will immediately skip the rest of the block and jump to the following catch block to be processed. In this case, the catch block isn't doing anything, so we're ignoring errors completely. This is a bad idea because if something goes wrong, we have no way of knowing.

Now look at this:

```
1   callApi(function(result) {
2     if (result.status !== 0) {
3       return
4     }
5
6     model.apiCall.success = true
7
8     if (result.data.items.length <= 0) {
9       return
10    }
11
12    model.apiCall.numOfItems = result.data.items.length
13
14    if (!isValid(result.data)) {
```

```
15      return
16    }
17
18    model.apiCall.result = result.data
19  })
```

That's a lot better. I removed the `try/catch` block, for starters (although it would have been equally good to properly handle and report the error). We can clearly see the "normal path" for the code to follow, and only in abnormal situations does the code stray off into an `if` block. Debugging is much simpler. And if we want to add extra code to handle error conditions, it will be easy to add a couple of lines inside those `if` blocks (imagine if the `if` blocks in the original code had `else` blocks attached! That would be so confusing).

7. Pure functions

A pure function (or functional method) is a function that does not alter or use external data (it's *stateless*). In other words, for a given input, it will always provide exactly the same output, no matter what has changed outside of it, and all your other variables will be completely unaffected by what happens inside of it. All pure functions have at least one argument and return at least one value.

This function is pure:

```
1  function getSumOfSquares(number1, number2) {
2    return Math.pow(number1, 2) + Math.pow(number2, 2)
3  }
```

And this one is not:

```
1  function getSumOfSquares() {
2    scope.sum = Math.pow(scope.number1, 2) + Math.pow(scope.number2, 2)
3  }
```

If you want to debug the first function, everything you need is right there in three lines of code. You can paste it into a separate environment, like jsfiddle[37] or the browser console, and play with it until you find out what's wrong.

If you want to debug the second function, you may have to dig through the entire program in order to make sure that you've found all the places where `scope.sum`, `scope.number1` and `scope.number2` are accessed. And if you ever want to move the function to another class or file, you'll have to worry about whether it has access to all the same data.

Not all methods can be pure; if your application didn't have state, its usefulness would be limited. But you should write pure functions often. This will make your program easy to maintain and scale.

---

[37]https://jsfiddle.net/

8. Automated tests

An automated test is a piece of code that executes another piece of code and checks the results to make sure it's working. This is much faster and more reliable than trying to test every feature of the app on your own every time you make a change. Every major programming language has tools and libraries to help you write these tests. Some are called *unit tests*, which test a small, self-contained piece of code (like a class or method), and others are *integration tests*, which test the way different pieces of code interact.

Writing automated tests for your own code is considered an essential part of being an effective programmer. Any class or method that's more than a bare wrapper over other code—that is, any class or method that contains logic—should be accompanied by a unit test. That unit test should run automatically whenever your team merges code to the main branch.

Unit tests, properly written, weed out false assumptions and make your code easier to understand. If someone doesn't know what a piece of code does, they can look at the unit test and see use cases. Writing tests can be tedious, and there's such a thing as too many tests, but if you ever go into a task thinking, *wow, this one's tricky*, that's a sure sign that you should be writing tests along the way.

Conclusion

Good code is a joy to maintain, build upon, and solve problems with. Bad code is painful to work with. Choose to write good code; you'll thank yourself for it.

A good question to ask yourself when writing code is: will this be easy to delete when we don't need it any more? If it's deeply nested, copied-and-pasted all over the place, dependent on various levels of state and lines of code throughout the program, and otherwise confusing, people will be unable to understand its purpose and impact and they'll be uncomfortable deleting it. But if it's immediately clear how it's used and what other code it interacts with, people will be able to delete it confidently when its usefulness runs out. I know you love your code, but the truth is that the world will be better off without it someday. And that's okay.

Programming tools

Gianluca Fiore

In your climb to the highest peaks of the programming world, hopefully you will encounter a plethora of languages, resources, conversations, and people. All of them will be accessible to you through *tools*, whether they be a web browser, an editor, a compiler or something else, depending on the task at hand. The choice of what tool to use for a given job may be daunting at the beginning and is one you shouldn't waste too much precious time on—that time is best spent actually learning and coding. This chapter will help you to understand how important your choice of tools for coding is, or is not, and why so many programmers care a great deal about theirs.

Programming is luckily extremely forgiving of not choosing the best tool for a specific task, especially for advanced programmers who have learned how to "bend" tools and languages to their will. Yet at the beginning a poor tool for what you're trying to achieve could make you waste a lot of time and possibly give up altogether. Please don't.

The tool of choice will depend on your area of expertise. If you are doing front end web programming, the choice of browser you're developing on first is vital, since they differ in the features and development tools they support; a back end programmer may care more about a good debugger and compiler, if any, and so on.

Every programming language has its strengths and weaknesses. Some are truly fast, like C, but ask you to do more math and be more careful with possible bugs in your code. Others are much easier, like Python and Ruby, but will usually be slower unless heavily optimized—something that, at the beginning, may be hard to master. If you need to write a website nowadays JavaScript is king so trying to do it with a language not specifically designed for the web, like Go or Java, might increase the difficulty for you. You could still do it, sure, but very few beginning programmers have the knowledge to depart from the specific goal that a programming language was designed for.

Thus, it's best to focus on what your project needs to achieve and what you would like your path in the programming world to be and choose the right language for them. You will learn faster and will meet less difficulties with your projects. There is always time to learn other languages later and to expose yourself to their new concepts. No language is useless to learn. But don't try to learn language X because Y is using it and it sounds cool. Learn what is useful for you.

The same is valid for operating systems and editors. Pick the tool you feel most productive and comfortable in. It may not be the best operating system ever nor the one with the best tools or the editor that will make you type fastest, but it's more important to get started and not waste time fighting against the tool to make it behave like you want. There's no need to make it more complicated than it should be.

Wars? What wars?

Related to this, if you follow news or discussions about programming on social media or online groups you may be surprised to find that the word "war" is used when discussing various tools.

It may be an "editor war" or "browser war" or the "tabs vs spaces" war. Or the "OSes war", which stands for "Operating Systems war". They are not actual wars fought with weapons and soldiers, luckily, but with words and interminable discussions on which tool is the best for a specific job or task, or about which one is simply better or whether you should code in a specific way or not. These "wars" date back decades, a few even before some of us were born, and show no signs of ever ending in a truce.

So what are those wars then? And why should you care (or not)?

The origin of it all lays in the tendency of many programmers of average or high experience to stick with a system, be it a language, a framework, or a tool, throughout their career—either because it is the one they like the best, they find themselves the most comfortable coding with or in it, or simply because it was the first one they truly mastered and don't feel like learning a new one. There's absolutely nothing wrong with that and it's part of the reason some languages have had such a long life despite tens of newer languages having been developed after them.

In any case, some programmers may seem outraged that you use, let's say, Windows instead of MacOS. Or that you chose to start coding with a visual code editor like Atom or Visual Studio instead of a text-based editor like Emacs or Vim. Or that your personal browser of choice doesn't appeal to them because it's not up to date with modern web standards or is developed by EvilCompany™ and by using it you are contributing to their world dominance plans or something.

These are the "wars" you will definitely hear about. Some people will try to convince you to use a different tool for your job, for practical or ideological reasons. Even ethical ones, sometimes. Whatever you may think about them, they're part of the history of computing and are part of the folklore, along with countless jokes and memes, of the programming community as a whole. Knowing a bit about them will help you navigate the references that may occasionally pop up in threads on social media and forums and help you choose the right tools at the beginning of your programming journey.

The ancient editor war

One of the most famous, and still going strong, is the religious war between Emacs and Vim ("religious" as there actually is a Church Of Emacs, no joke). For those who don't know them well, Emacs and Vim are two ancient text editors that over the years have developed a vast community around them, with thousands of plugins to increase their functionality and an array of different themes to change their appearance. If you haven't had the chance to read their history yet, Vim stands for "Vi Improved" as it is the direct successor of a previous editor, Vi, which in turn was inspired by an even older one, Ed. We're talking early 70s here. Bram Moolenaar, the author of Vim, ported it to various platforms and made it "modern" in its functionality for that time. Curiously,

Emacs was also indirectly inspired by Ed as its ancestor was TECO, which was similar to the Ed editor. Later Richard Stallman improved it (see the pattern?) and renamed it Editor Macros, Emacs for short. End of history lesson.

On the deepest level, the rivalry between the 2 editors is not a practical one: they both do their job very well, in our case allowing us to code in an efficient way, and are great at not overwhelming a new programmer with too many features—you won't feel too lost at first as you can just learn what you need to start coding without getting lost in a ton of menus and options. Actually, in their text versions, neither has any menus at all.

Where they do differ is in the philosophy: Vim espouses the *small is beautiful* and *do one thing well* tenets of the system it was originally developed for, Unix, while Emacs centers on supporting development as an entire operational hub. Emacs tries to be the center of your coding experience, providing you with all the features you need to develop with ease, whereas Vim tries to just edit text very well and lets you add other features with plugins. Emacs is all-encompassing, Vim is more focused. Both are very quirky by today's standards and may seem extremely counterintuitive at first. That in turn gives rise to a smaller "war" between those preferring more modern coding environments, graphical ones usually, and those that stuck with Emacs or Vim.

The point of this particular war is how one prefers to code: with a single program, which you probably never leave and contains all your code, debugger and text editing capabilities, or with multiple programs that you open from time to time, when you need, and can keep in the background of your work, occupying less hardware resources at the cost of being more minimal. Whether you prefer one philosophy or another, or want to totally avoid both Emacs and Vim, it's not important when you are starting out as a coder. Your focus should be on learning to code. You will develop preferences for one mainstream philosophy or another, or perhaps even develop your own alternative, in the future. Right now these editors are just tools that can help you code better, not necessarily faster. If you don't feel at ease with them, postpone learning them until later. Stick to solving problems and completing code projects, not getting to know all the idiosyncrasies of various editors. If you prefer a beginner-friendly interface, editors like Atom or Visual Studio Code will make you feel at home.

The Windows/Linux war

The same attitude can be held regarding the OS wars too. There are plenty of opinionated programmers that will swear by using Windows or MacOS, and others that will laugh at them as the "real" coding experience can be had only with more minimal, "barebone" operating systems like Linux[38] and BSD[39]. Either can be right of course, this isn't the book to discuss which operating system is the best for programming. The best one for you is the one that allows you to be the most productive, that gets least in the way of your learning and improving as a programmer. If you are already using one that you feel perfectly comfortable with, have no grudge against and have perhaps explored a few alternatives but none have sparked any interest, keep using your current operating

---

[38]https://en.wikipedia.org/wiki/Linux
[39]https://en.wikipedia.org/wiki/Berkeley_Software_Distribution

system. Don't get bogged down in perfecting what already works. The tools are for you to use and if you aren't more productive with a commonly reputed "better" one, stick with the one you have.

Browser and style wars

Of a slightly different nature, and here is where you should start to care more, are the "tabs vs spaces" war and the browser war. The latter is easier to understand so let's start there. If you are heading towards being a front end web developer, you may already know that different browsers have different rendering engines—how they create the actual pieces that a webpage is composed of, and render or "show" them on the screen. That (as a really simplified explanation) is what browsers do, they take instructions in the form of HTML, CSS or JavaScript code and process them through their internal engine to produce a visual result, a webpage that can be read and interacted with by users. Having different engines, the process by which they render the webpage is different and thus the results can be different too. That means a webpage can look different depending on what browser you use to access it. The same is true for mobile devices: a webpage is shown in a different way depending on the size of the device the browser is installed on. That's a well-known fact and an intentional feature meant to adapt any webpage to any device, from the tiniest cell phones to the largest quad-monitor setups.

The browser wars were born out of different browsers competing to capture the widest audience; in ancient times they were sold on CDs and thus they had to be commercially successful. Nowadays all browsers are free to download (except for Safari that is only available for Apple machines) and the commercial incentive is not directly money but instead related to the rendering engines: if a browser becomes so widespread that it has an absolute majority of the internet users, then it is easier for developers to write their webpages targeting only its rendering engine, making sure it looks the best on it and not considering minimal differences in appearance with other browsers. Thus, indirectly, a browser that has a dominant share of the market can influence the development of the technologies that compose the Web by implementing some of them earlier, or not implementing others at all, knowing that many developers will follow their lead.

Over the course of the last 30 years since the Web was born, various browsers have reached a dominant status over the others. Netscape, Internet Explorer, Firefox, and Chrome have all had their share of the spotlight in these browser wars. Regardless of the reasons why each browser rose and fell, what's important to us as developers is that using one browser over the others will mean not only having different tools for development (usually called "Dev Tools" or "Developer Tools"), but running the risk of optimizing the websites we write for that browser and that browser only. It's way too common to be lazy and content with your website looking good on your browser of choice, assuming that it's okay for others too. Or, worse, noticing some small issue with the layout or an oversized font or a slightly misplaced menu in another browser and ignoring it because "only a few people use it". That may be true, but if not, its users won't have a good experience using the site and this will increase the feeling that the most widespread browser is the "best" one. You are indirectly and involuntarily creating a monopoly in the browser market. This is why I try to make sure I test my webpages with all major browsers at the very least. If we keep the competition open and fair, developers and users alike will benefit from it.

"Tabs vs spaces" is a more technical war. In the beginning, talking again of the early 70s, editors would use a tab character to indent code. One tab character was the equivalent of eight space characters and in the old days disk space was scarce, so one character was better than eight. Nowadays we have disks in the order of terabytes so the difference is negligible. Yet the issue here is of interoperability: Mac and Windows editors tend to make a tab character the equivalent of four spaces while on Linux and BSD, it is still eight. Unless you change the preference in your editor of choice, of course. Because of this, most fans of spaces instead of tabs will consider you wrong for using tabs because a space character is always a space character, no matter the editor and system you are using. On the other hand, tab fans claim that one tab is much less typing than four to eight spaces.

The issue is, if you are using four spaces, for instance, and your programming buddy uses eight, then the code will be indented differently and some languages, like Python, will even bail out with errors as the syntax of the language depends on the correct indentation of the code. And besides, the resulting code will look messy and hard to read. Moreover, copying and pasting from a web browser in a local editor will most definitely screw up the indentation as it will depend on which browser, which website, which editor and which operating system you are copying and pasting from/to. There's far from a standard here.

So for portability, do consider what you prefer and stick to it, but not before having spent a little bit of time to check what is the recommended way to indent in your programming language and in the project you are coding on. There are guidelines about tabs vs spaces in all the most popular languages. It will make everybody's life easier and save you from arguing with older programmers that will most surely believe their stance in this war is the "right" one.

Use what you like, focus on learning

In an ideal world, nobody would judge you because you have taken a specific stance in one of these wars (or not) or because of your choice of tools. Some will joke about it and some will fake being offended that you have a different opinion, but nobody should discriminate against you in your path to becoming a good programmer, just because you use a specific editor or prefer a Mac to a PC. Yet it will happen, so it's important to be at least aware of each of these wars. They may influence your choice of coding tools. And hopefully this bit of history will save you from endless discussions about which side is right, if any. As Bertrand Russell famously said, "War does not determine who is right—only who is left."

You are an interpreter

Edaqa Mortoray

Programming is primarily about translation. You take the desires of a user and translate them into source code. It's a process requiring a strong understanding of technology, the users, and all the people involved in development.

I know a lot of you may wish to keep your head in the code, but becoming a great programmer depends on you becoming a great mediator. Imagination far outpaces our current technology, leading to extreme mismatches in what users expect and what our computers can actually do. As a programmer, you'll be required to temper those expectations and produce a nonetheless desirable product.

You'll need to empathize with the user and consult with colleagues on their views. Development is not a process that can be done by one person. Programmers represent the technology, which is a cornerstone to the process, but still only one part. Our products entirely hinge on the software doing something useful, but without teamwork working towards a shared vision, that'll never happen.

Soft skills is often the term used to refer to this part of the job—interacting productively with users and teammates in pursuit of a common goal. I don't know if that term accurately represents this skill set. The ability to communicate is an *essential* skill. Your ability to get inside the user's head is critical to the success of the project. The importance of you as a translator and mediator of technology cannot be overstated.

Nobody cares about your code

Let's back up for a second, and start at the code. While it is only part of our job, it is the domain where a programmer's presence dominates. We own this artifact of development. It is our responsibility to create it, and we have to address all issues with the code.

The ability to write code is a significant competence that all programmers must develop. There is no way you can translate requests into code if you don't know how to write it. Your ability to translate is limited by your vocabulary.

Imagine having to work with somebody who doesn't share a language with you—say someone who only speaks Italian, while you only speak English. You'd need an interpreter that can translate for you. The quality of the translation is limited by the interpreter's understanding of both English *and* Italian. If they can speak only a bit of Italian, their interpretation won't be natural, and your Italian colleague will have a hard time understanding what you meant to say. Similarly, it doesn't help if the translator speaks Italian fluently but is weak with English. The translator can formulate great sentences in Italian, but potentially from a misunderstanding of what you said.

In programming, you are an interpreter who must speak two languages. Code is one of the languages you need to speak. But you also need to speak the language of users and other developers in your company. It's irrelevant that you weave wondrous structures of code if you've misunderstood what you're supposed to be building. It's also pointless if you're a master empath, and you can understand the user perfectly, but you can't figure out how to express that in code.

Source code is a work artifact. It's there to support the high-level goals of the product. Ultimately, other than you and a few other programmers on your team, nobody cares about the code. It's all about the product. The user cares about what you've built and how it solves their problem, not so much about how you got there. Knowing this improves the appreciation of your work, and lets you make the right decisions.

Sharing the journey of the user

But what goals does the code need to support? Here we look to the users of the products: the people that will be installing the app on their phone, going to your web page, or downloading a desktop program. Understanding the people using our software is the highest priority of development. The user experience is our utmost goal.

You may have already heard about user stories, journeys, and personas. These are all tools that capture what the user wants. They should be used on most projects. It's actually hard to avoid them. Even if you don't use a strict method or have rigid formality, you will be considering the user's wishes in your project. Learning user tools, such as user stories and portraits, makes the process easier and more robust. But just like code, they are not the purpose of the project.

The purpose of user portraits and stories is to keep the focus on the user. A portrait tells us what job a user has, where they live, and what their goals are in life. We create these descriptions to better empathize with people using our product. If these people remain nameless and abstract, it's easy to forget about who they are.

Having a bit of formality, such as writing down our ideas, allows us to communicate with other teams. It's more comfortable to talk to other departments in the domain of the user than of technology. By talking about the product from the user's viewpoint, we stick to a universal language that everybody can understand.

This is more challenging than talking about code. Code has a strict structure and lack of ambiguity. By contrast, human language is full of amorphous thoughts and wandering ideas. It's this lack of clarity that causes most issues within development. But as difficult as it may be, getting all departments to talk in the language of the user is worth it. It's how great software is made.

Much like the code isn't the product, the product isn't actually what the user wants. People have real-world tasks they wish to perform. They are willing to use a tool to get them done, but that's all it is: a means to an end. They may not even know what kind of tool they need (see Appendix A, "XY Problem"). This is why it's essential to talk in the language of the user, not the product. This subtle distinction in wording shifts the emphasis of development from technical requirements to user expectations.

For example, most people don't want a car for the purpose of having a car. Many people don't even want to drive, but they have a car to get to other locations. These drivers care primarily about how they get somewhere with their vehicle. All the polish and extra features are pointless if it's hard to get somewhere. This is why things like public transit and taxis compete in the same market. When stating requirements, there's a significant difference between "wanting to own a car," and "wanting to travel between locations."

As another example, we have apps that allow us to organize events, from large to small. As the developer, you must keep in mind that the users are trying to hold an event. Your app is strictly a tool the organizer and attendees will use. Adding features that don't support the event organizers may at best be ignored by the user, and at worst get in the way. I'm sure we can all think of numerous apps that have nonsensical features in them.

Everything and yet nothing we want

Ensuring our high-level requirements stay in the domain of our users addresses a fundamental problem. Technology can't do everything. Indeed, it doesn't come anywhere close to all the things we want to do. It can neither do them the way we want to do them nor understand what we actually want to do. Despite the extreme reliance we have on computers, they are still constrained when compared to all that is possible.

People's desires are not limited by technology. Their imagination shows no bounds. The expectations placed on technology tend to grow faster than technology itself advances. The demands placed on our computers, our gadgets, our networks, increase at alarming rates.

It's your job as a programmer to translate these unbound ideas into the limited space of what computers can actually do.

Losing track of the user's desires means you run the risk of working on the wrong things. While computers are limited in fulfilling user desires, they are unbound in their own domain. There's a wide variety of interesting, cool, and clever things we get a computer to do. It's easy to go down the road of technical beauty and stray far from the goals of the project.

Your focus on the user is what keeps you on track. For every line of code you write, for each module you install, for every host you deploy, you should be thinking about why the user needs this. If you're unable to draw a clear connection from your work to those high-level user goals, then something is wrong.

Part of a larger development community

This focus on the user isn't only for programmers. No project can be done by programmers alone. Beyond the users, there are numerous other departments in a development company—designers, product owners, project managers, executives, quality assurance, and so on. You have to be able to converse with all of them about the product. You need to all be working towards a shared vision.

When somebody is left out of the process two things happen. First, their ideas, concerns, and requirements will be lost. This could result in a product of lower quality. Second, they feel marginalized and may become demotivated. Continuing in that state, they may become bitter and angry.

Tensions between teams are unfortunately all too familiar. A lot of this tension comes from people not properly communicating. While two teams may both fully believe in the product, an inability to share that vision can lead to hostility.

This discord can rapidly foment an unpleasant workplace. Nobody, including you, wants that. You work there, so keeping everything pleasant is in your best interest.

When things turn sour, productivity suffers. Not only are people, including you, demotivated, but they also end up working on the wrong things. The vision of the product becomes blurred, and ultimately it will fail. Instead of working together, everybody starts complaining about the other teams, how they don't listen and don't understand.

Always remember, communication is a two-way street. The best way to be misunderstood by someone is by not talking to them. The best way to misunderstand someone is to close your ears to them.

As technology and time are limited, development is all about compromise. Not everything can be done. You, as a programmer, represent the technical side of the equation and must bring that knowledge to the negotiating table. Learn when to speak up and how to bring your concerns to the table.

If you can't build a particular feature, you must make that clear. If you have an idea for a feature that you think would help the user, but that nobody has mentioned yet, you should bring it up. If teams have requests for features that would help them and cost little, it's worthwhile to implement them to improve relations. If a high-visibility defect isn't getting fixed, you need to explain why that is.

Your prioritization process must be transparent, or tension will build. People are better able to accept the rejection of their ideas if they understand why they are being rejected. When people share a user-focused vision of the product, it's easier to identify high impact items and work on them first.

Deserving of trust and autonomy

By having open processes and taking the time to listen to other teams, you'll build trust between each other. We rely on other teams to do their job. Just as we translate others' wishes into code, our own requirements will be converted into work processes in various teams. A request for artwork will be taken by a graphic artist and turned into images. We may ask marketing about our target user, and they'll come back with a persona. We have some idea of what they're doing, but the details of their work aren't our concern.

Development is not an exact science, and we all need room to maneuver if we're to get the system right. This is why it's crucial that requirements stay in the realm of users. The internals of the software must be flexible.

If requirements specify how a system should work internally, they interfere with the job of the programmer. The same goes for other departments. We aren't going to tell the graphics team what Photoshop layering technique they should be using, nor will we specify which ERP accounts the finance team should create to handle microtransactions. All teams have an expected amount of autonomy to perform their work.

This autonomy is based on everybody having a shared vision. We are all allowed, and expected, to contribute to the product's goals. That shared user domain is everybody's responsibility. This goes hand-in-hand with trust. There's no way you can implement the system correctly if you don't know what those high-level goals are.

Your flexibility and trust in your work depend on your understanding of the user. And that's tied to how well you can communicate with other teams.

Becoming a great programmer

The emphasis for programming is often placed on coding. It's a comfortable place to start learning. Initially, it's likely the place where you lack the most skills. You've grown up in the real world, so to some degree, you've been working on your soft skills for years already.

Natural experience won't be enough, however. The particular skills needed for communication as a programmer require additional training. You need to take the time to learn the various techniques used for translating user desires into code.

Don't feel overwhelmed though. Nobody can naturally do everything, and it'll take time to learn both code and communication. You'll be part of teams that will help you along. You and your teammates will have strengths and weaknesses to compliment each other.

You won't always act on your own. If you're a junior programmer, it's vital to have a mentor that can help you along. It's expected that programming teams discuss how the code should work. It's important to have a good leader who can make good decisions, and when needed, state precisely how some system should work. The dynamics within a programming team differ; however, the dynamic is always based on communication. And you should never let anybody hide the user's wishes from you.

Becoming a great programmer is primarily about your ability to act as an interpreter. You can't be ultra-productive only by being awesome at coding. Productivity is about choosing the right things to work on and figuring out the best way to cover the product requirements. Your value will be measured by how well you appear to be supporting the company. The better you perform with other people, the better you can tailor your effort towards high impact items.

What to learn first

Isaac Lyman

I occasionally get a message from a brand-new developer who's overwhelmed by all the technologies and choices that exist in the world of software development. Where do you even start? Some of these devs have seen job advertisements like the following:

Core Requirements

- 3+ years experience as a full-stack or front-end web engineer
- Strong written and verbal communication skills
- Love of collaboration
- Deep knowledge of JavaScript (es6+), HTML, and CSS
- Experience with front-end build systems, especially Webpack
- Significant experience in at least one modern front-end framework (React, Angular, Vue.js)
- Experience in at least one modern back-end framework (Django, Rails, Spark, Express)

Bonus Experience

- Experience with TypeScript
- Experience with Vue.js
- Experience using Webpack to build Vue apps written in TypeScript
- Other experience in modern front-end devops
- Experience with WebGL, three.js, etc

This is for a standard, mid-level web development position. It lists 14 specific technologies, alludes to many more, and if that weren't enough, it has an "etc." Even as a senior software engineer, I'm not sure what that "etc." refers to. Maybe I could Google it:

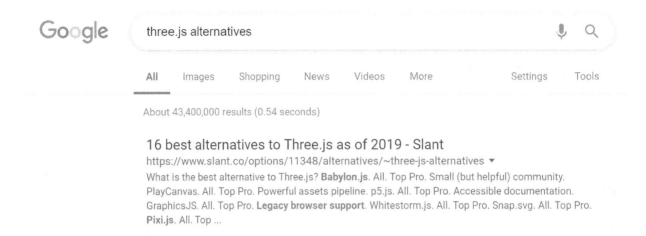

Oh, great. 16 more technologies. If I were brand-new to this, I'd be thinking, "you mean I have to learn 30 different programming languages just to get a mid-level job?" And then I'd throw up my hands and apply for a job in something less demanding, like brain surgery.

Let's put that fear to bed: no, you don't have to learn 30 different programming languages, now or ever. You need to learn one. Then you need to learn a few tools that are commonly used with that language. That will get you a junior position. Afterward, you've got options: get better and better with the languages and tools you already know (you might call this the "expert in the room" route), or learn several more (the "startup engineer" route). Either route will let you advance your career and make more money, and neither is necessarily better than the other, but you'll probably find that you strongly prefer one of them.

So where should you start?

Make a list of technologies you're considering. Then pick one, any way you like. If there's a company you want to work for and they recruit heavily for one of them, pick that one. Or if you know *what* you want to build, pick the tech that goes with it (see Appendix B for ideas). Or go with your gut. Or flip a coin, or roll a d20, or pick one out of a hat. There's no "best" technology. What's important here is that you *commit*. Spend time getting to know the technology, building simple projects with it, reading articles about it, finding GitHub repositories that use it.

Some people start second-guessing themselves after a day or two with a new technology, so they switch to a different one, and then another one, and then another. This is like learning to say "Good morning" in 50 different languages. It's a party trick, not a marketable skill. Don't let yourself do this. Even if you spend five years with something and decide it's not for you, it's not a total loss; 75% or more of the skills you've learned will transfer neatly to your next technology. The consequences of choosing the "wrong" technology are tiny.

If you don't know a programming language yet, I recommend starting with JavaScript, Python or C#. All of these are extremely popular and in high demand. If you already know JavaScript, learn a utility tool like Lodash and a web framework like React or Vue, or learn Node.js and a server-side framework like Express or Hapi. If you know Python, learn a data science library like NumPy or Pandas, or a web framework like Django or Flask. If you know C#, learn ASP.NET MVC to build web applications, Xamarin to build native apps, or Unity to build video games.

Once you've picked some technologies, the best thing you can do is *start a project* (see Leonóra's chapter "Making the most out of side projects"). Think up something small and simple you want to build, then put it together a step at a time, learning what you need to learn as you go along. This is the best way to gain competence. It doesn't much matter what you build, as long as it's interesting to you—to-do list apps are the cliche, but you could just as easily build a game, a unit conversion calculator, a chat room, a conversation bot, or anything else that comes to mind. The only limit is your imagination. For some free ideas, check out the graveyard tag[40] on dev.to, where several developers have written about the projects they've built on their own over the years.

Once you finish your project you'll have a nice portfolio piece, along with the confidence of knowing you can see a project through from start to finish. And you'll be well on your way to being an expert in the technology of your choice.

I promise, as long as you don't go out of your way to choose strange and obscure technologies, anything you choose can lead to a successful career. There are plenty of jobs out there waiting for you.

---

[40]https://dev.to/t/graveyard

Learning to learn

Yechiel Kalmenson

"You need to learn how to learn" is a phrase you will often hear as you start on your journey.

Don't worry about which language/framework resource X or course Y teaches, people will tell you, what's important is that they show you how to learn on your own.

There is truth to that. The majority of new developers don't get a job using the first stack they learned. Even if you are lucky enough to get a job using the frameworks you learned, the breakneck pace of the tech world virtually guarantees that your knowledge will be outdated in no time and you will have to learn the next shiny thing every few years.

Students who find themselves too focused on acquiring a particular technology, instead of focusing on acquiring the skills needed to keep learning on their own, might find themselves blindsided when tasked with learning a *different* technology just to get their first junior role. They may feel like the experience they gained at their bootcamp or college (or the resources they spent self-teaching) was a waste of time and money.

Changing your perspective from thinking that you need to learn Ruby, or JavaScript, or React, or what have you, to realizing that you are really trying to learn *how to learn* those skills will leave you better prepared for the task of finding your first job as a developer and for the lifetime of learning and growth that will follow. Not to mention that it will help you learn whatever technology it is that you decided to go with first more effectively.

But what does it mean to "learn how to learn"? What are the skills that developers use to help them keep up with a never-ending stream of new frameworks and technologies?

After many conversations with both former and potential students and career changers, I believe I was able to narrow it down to four skills that you need to acquire if you want to be able to learn on your own after graduating:

1. How to read and understand error messages.
2. How to Google things.
3. How to read and understand technical documentation.
4. How and when to take a step back and ask for help.

From my experience as a developer, I can say that I spend 90% of my workday doing one of those four things. If you can master these skills, you can be reasonably confident that there is no technology you can't pick up.

Reading error messages

This was one of the first lessons I had to learn when learning to code, and, in my opinion, what separates developers from the rest of society.

Back in my "civilian life" error messages were scary, they were opaque, they felt like the computer was screaming at me in a foreign language and blaming me for something which it probably thought was my fault.

When I started learning how to code I naturally ran into many error messages, and that felt very discouraging; I felt like I must be doing something wrong.

Then one day it "clicked" for me. I was watching a lecture by one of the bootcamp instructors where he was coding an app. At one point he ran the code and hit an error and instead of getting embarrassed or flustered he exclaimed, completely unironically, "We hit an error! Great!" That's when I realized that error messages are far from our enemies. When we encounter an error message as developers, it's the computer's way of letting us know what's wrong with our code; it's how it provides clues on what we need to fix.

As a developer, you will be working exclusively with broken code (if the code already works then who needs you?). Reading and analyzing error messages is how you will go about fixing it.

The kinds of error messages you get and how helpful they are will depend a lot on which language/framework you are using. Some languages have more helpful errors than others, but some elements are universal.

Every error message will usually contain:

1. The error message: what actually went wrong. These can vary from a few cryptic words to a full paragraph containing suggestions on what you might be able to do to fix the bug.
2. The location where the error occurred: the file, line number, and sometimes the function name where your program was when it crashed.

3. The stack trace: all the lines in your code that the program executed until getting to the function in number 2. This can help trace where your function was called and with which parameters.

Reading all that and getting comfortable with parsing the different parts of the error message can take some practice, but that's the first place to look when your code doesn't behave the way you expect it to.

A good bootcamp or Computer Science course will encourage you to play around with the code and break things, and will celebrate error messages instead of just showing you how to fix them.

But error messages, helpful as they are, are limited in how much they can help you. After all, the designers of the language can't know in advance *all* of the different ways programs written in their language can break. That's when the next skill comes in handy.

How to Google stuff

As a developer, you will spend the majority of the time doing things you don't know by heart. Google (or DuckDuckGo, Bing, etc.) will be your best friend.

For beginners, it can be hard to know what to Google for, especially in the beginning when you aren't even sure what it is you're trying to do, never mind verbalize it in a way that a search engine can understand. Learning how to structure your query for best results is an art that comes with experience, but some rules will help you get started:

- Include the language you are using: if you are learning Ruby and have an array you want to sort, searching for "how to sort an array" will probably not be very helpful; when I just did it the first page of results contained only answers about how to do it in Java, Visual Basic, and JavaScript. Always start your query with the name of the language you are searching for (in our example, "ruby sort an array" will give you plenty of results that a Ruby programmer would actually find useful).

- Use well-defined keywords: this comes more with experience, but knowing which keywords represent the actual information you need will save you time filtering through unhelpful results. As a general rule, don't include words that aren't necessary; crafting the shortest query that contains all the keywords relevant to your search will help make sure that you get only the results you want.

- Know which results are more likely to be helpful: again, this comes with experience, but some results are more likely to be useful than others. You will develop a taste for this with time, but in general, more recent results are less likely to be out of date, and an answer on Stack Overflow with a hundred upvotes is more likely to be helpful than a blog-post from a no-name author (which isn't to say there aren't great blog-posts by relatively unknown authors).

This last point brings us to the next skill.

How to read technical documentation

Languages/frameworks have many features and functions, and unless you use a particular function on a semi-regular basis, it is unlikely that you will have the syntax memorized.

This doesn't mean that you are a lousy programmer. Even accomplished programmers with many years of experience find themselves Googling things like "concatenate a string" or "filter an array."

 **DHH** ✓
@dhh

 Following ⌄

Hello, my name is David. I would fail to write bubble sort on a whiteboard. I look code up on the internet all the time. I don't do riddles.

2:04 PM - 21 Feb 2017

Source: https://twitter.com/dhh/status/834146806594433025?lang=en[41]. *DHH is the founder of Basecamp and the creator of Ruby on Rails, one of the most popular frameworks for web development.*

The documentation for most languages is usually the most comprehensive and concise reference for language features, saving you the trouble of memorizing hundreds of obscure language features.

---

[41]https://twitter.com/dhh/status/834146806594433025?lang=en

For example, Ruby has about 20 different ways to iterate over an array. If you are trying to learn Ruby, you might think that you have to memorize all 20, but if your goal is to learn how to learn then all you have to remember is that you can find all the ways of iterating over an array in the documentation on Ruby's Enumerable module[42].

The problem for beginners is that the documentation can look dense and intimidating; its conciseness means that the page can look like a scary wall of jargon and technical terms and symbols, but with practice, you can learn the patterns and learn how to find the information you need. With time you will see that the official docs will become your go-to reference for simple syntax.

Ask for help

Finally, there is another very crucial skill that is not exactly about self-learning, but it's an essential skill to have if you want to be an effective learner.

Photo: WOCinTech Chat[43]. Unmodified image licensed under CC BY 2.0[44]

The last skill is knowing when to step back and ask for help.

None of us ever did it on our own; the "self-taught developer" is a myth.

[42]https://ruby-doc.org/core-2.6.1/Enumerable.html
[43]https://www.flickr.com/photos/136629440@N06/25392428253
[44]https://creativecommons.org/licenses/by/2.0/deed.en

Surrounding yourself with a network of mentors and fellow learners, and knowing when/how to leverage said network, will save you time best spent actually learning new things. It will mean that you don't have to spend hours banging your head against the keyboard over a simple typo that a second, fresh pair of eyes would have caught right away (though we've all been there).

There are many online communities geared at beginners. If you are in a bootcamp they probably have ways for students (both current and former) to connect. Dev Twitter is extremely friendly, helpful, and supportive (some of my favorite communities are the #CodeNewbie[45] community and @ThePracticalDev[46]). Find your corner, your people you connect with, and you will see that traveling together is 100 times better than traveling alone.

In conclusion

In conclusion, learning to code is a big decision. Many factors are involved in what makes a good bootcamp, course, or resource. I hope that reading this chapter will give you an idea of which skills are essential to focus on and which are just a passing fad.

Good luck!

---

[45]https://twitter.com/CodeNewbies
[46]https://twitter.com/ThePracticalDev

Make the most of side projects

Leonóra Dér

This chapter will be about side projects and I would like to convince all of you that they are great!

So what comes to your mind when I say "side projects"?

Maybe you know of CommitStrip. It's a blog about the daily life of developers and I just love reading their stuff, but one of my favorite strips[47] from them is about side projects. It shows a very typical situation: a developer having millions of unfinished, never-going-to-end projects. Have you ever felt like this? Not yet?

In some ways I'm writing to motivate you to do this. To start new side projects. To also finish them, of course, but to be able to finish one, first you have to start it! But why would anyone want to do that?

Famous examples

To get an idea of what side projects really are, first check out a few famous ones. I guess I have to start with a couple of the most famous side projects, Gmail and AdSense. Both were created by enthusiastic Googlers.

Twitter, ProductHunt and even GitHub were once side projects. And the list of side projects that became million-dollar startups goes on...

My projects

But don't tune out just yet! You might think that I'm crazy about side projects and the truth is, I am. I'd like to show you a few of my own side projects so you can see how they've helped me. I picked very different ones:

The very first of my side projects was an online tool where you could create, edit, and share a business model. I used this project as an opportunity to learn Vue.js (a web framework) and Spring Boot (a Java server framework). Now, I've struggled to find users, but I recently made some progress: I spoke with a startup incubator who said they would love to use it! I'm more than happy with that. If you'd like to take a look, you can find it online[48]!

My current project is a challenge for developers. It will be a collection of challenges soon, but at the moment there is only one. It's called the Cretan Maze. You're trapped in a maze and have to get out,

---

[47]http://www.commitstrip.com/en/2014/11/25/west-side-project-story/
[48]http://businessmodelcanvas.io

but you have to collect three gold coins first and you control the game through a REST API. So as a developer you have to write a program to find your way out of the maze. I shared it on a few sites when I finished coding it. To tell the truth, it was a bit like testing in production. I mean…I checked the functions, everything was working properly more or less, but when a lot of people started to use it, bugs came out immediately. So I learned that I should conduct a beta test before I let everyone in through the front door. Anyway, you can try your hand at the challenge here[49].

Last but not least, the project I am most proud of is my blog. It's a blog for software developers, written in Hungarian. It is called 'fejlesztő lány' and I started it as a personal challenge; I needed something in my life I would have to spend at least 10-20 minutes with daily so I can keep track of the days. It might sound a bit weird, but sometimes I lose track of time. This blog and Facebook have helped me a lot and I know it's not a traditional side project, but I truly recommend to any developer to start a blog!

Cons

Now that we have an idea of what a side project can be, let's ask an obvious question: Why would anyone want to spend time on a side project?

I mean, you might say that you don't have time. I guess most of you have full-time jobs. You could say that after working for eight hours you are tired and you don't care at all. Or you have a family you would prefer to spend time with, and on the weekends you want to be far away from the keyboard, hiking in the mountains or playing on your local football team.

But remember, people say that you have time for what you make time for. I know it's a cliche but it is very true. Once I read a post by a dad who learned how to program in the evenings, and couldn't even sleep much as he had a newborn daughter to look after, but a few months later he got his very first developer job.

Think about that for a second. He put his time into it and he got a reward: a job offer. Sounds great, doesn't it?

You might also say that side projects are something that no one pays for, and no one will praise you for the effort and time you put into a side project if you fail or abandon it. The bitter truth is, undoubtedly, most side projects will fail. We all know this. The majority of them don't even reach the first release, and those that do often become abandonware, no longer supported by the developer. GitHub is a graveyard for them.

You could also say that it's useless to spend time on this stuff, creating another note-taking app, an alternative to one used by millions or billions of people, whatever for?

Pros

Let me show you all the advantages!

---

[49]https://coding-challanges.herokuapp.com/challanges/maze

The first advantage I'd like to emphasize is learning new technologies and dev skills.

For example, if you're a Java coder, why not try Python with a data science side project? Or if you're a backend developer, why don't you try out a shiny new frontend framework? Or let's say you usually do coding stuff, but deploying your own app to Heroku and setting up a database, Jenkins jobs, or code analysis with SonarQube could be a challenge for you!

We live in a world with constantly changing technologies. So if you want to keep up with the new trends, the best tool for the job is side projects, making some useless or not-so-useless projects to try out a new library, framework or tool.

Instead of staying updated on the latest frontend frameworks in the JavaScript universe, you could also have a project focused on learning how to write clean code, how to refactor legacy code, or how to do Test-Driven Development, because these things take a lot of time to master. You could try reading a well-known book on the topic and implementing the knowledge at the same time.

Another great benefit of side projects is that you are practising outside of your office hours. If you use the same technologies at work and for your hobby projects, you'll meet the most typical bugs and pitfalls beforehand so that you can feel more confident at work. You'll get to know the best practices, so you can help others make better decisions or give advice on using library A rather than library B, saving time for you and money for your company.

The next advantage I'd like to mention here is simply the joy of building something. It's fulfilling when you can show your product to others, or take a look at something and know you're the one that created it. You should be proud of yourself if you've completed a project that others can use or download. The feeling when other people are happily using your product is quite satisfying.

And there's another skill that you can build using your old side projects: refactoring. Think about it as working on legacy code that you have to make work by turning buggy, vulnerable code into something beautiful, making changes line by line, starting small but making powerful improvements in the long run.

Side projects are also great because they look great on your CV or resume. During the interview, when they ask about projects you've worked on, you'll be happily saying that you did this, that and some other stuff too. They help build your online presence and that certainly won't do any harm to your CV, career, network, or professional growth either.

If one of your projects gets serious then you can even quit your job, start a business, and become an entrepreneur. I'm not encouraging you to quit your job right now, but it might happen...

A friend of mine always says that a good side project makes you money while you sleep. But sometimes that mentality can do harm, as some people get very anxious when their projects start to make even a little money. Generally, the primary goal is not to make money, but to learn, to advance, to grow.

I have a few more advantages of side projects to share with you. For example, if you collaborate on an open source project or build something for a community, then you will be able to connect with developers from all around the world and make some new friends and connections. That sounds good, doesn't it?

Also, it's refreshing. It's a great way to get out of your comfort zone and do something different from your day job.

Last but not least, I would say that it's FUN! Think about it! You have the freedom to do whatever you want—there's no boss or client to tell you what to do and how to do it! You don't have to spend hours in useless meetings. You don't have to convince anybody of your own point of view. Your code will be super consistent and strictly follow all the best code conventions: yours.

How

Now that you know all the advantages and disadvantages of side projects, I would like to give you some advice on how to get the most of the time you're willing to spend on them.

Step 1: Find a topic

Usually when I want to learn a new technology, I build something. Getting your hands dirty is the only way of actually making sure that you got it right. You need those "aha!" moments you can't have just by reading or watching tutorials. A lot of people build "To Do List" apps, which are nice because they're easy to get started with and everyone is familiar with them. But I personally don't want to make yet another To Do app! If I'm going to spend my super precious time on something, I want to be making something that has a chance of creating value for someone. For me it's best to make something useful, but of course sometimes it's nice to do something just for fun.

Another suggestion: use a note-taking app. Ideas can come anytime, so be prepared! Otherwise you will forget them.

If you are clueless as to what to do, you can find millions of ideas on the internet!

Step 2: Make a plan

Don't worry, I'm not saying that you should start by writing a detailed, 100-page document. I'd guess you're used to that because of your day job. Your plan can be a random text file a few lines long, with core features, goals and milestones. It's usually useful to make separate files for the first version of the project and for changes, new features, etc. And don't forget to limit the scope and set a deadline!

Step 3: Find a community

You can find online forums and groups that are made for sharing and receiving constructive feedback on side projects. One of my favorites is the r/SideProject subreddit[50]. It's very active and well-moderated and you can even get some new ideas from there or use it for brainstorming.

---

[50]https://www.reddit.com/r/SideProject/

Step 4: Build something minimal, and I mean minimal

Believe me: even if you are an experienced developer, chances are that you're going to overestimate your own capacity. It's common to feel like you're more productive alone than you are inside your organization, and this is true to a certain extent. But if you don't keep your feature list short enough, chances are that you won't finish the project before you lose your motivation and interest.

Step 5: Become a finisher!

Despite your best intentions, things will come up. You'll always have good reasons not to finish a project, like going on holiday, taking German lessons, or reading funny stuff on the internet. But sometimes you have to say to yourself, "Hey, you are going to finish this app and put it on the Android app store. It doesn't matter how long it takes, you are going to work on this app at least an hour each day until it's done."

Step 6: Go live!

Going live isn't just about publishing your app to the app store or deploying your website to the web. It can be publishing a library to npm or even just open sourcing the code so people can see it, use it and learn from it. Don't forget to spread the word! Post about it on your blog, subreddits, dev communities, even ProductHunt. You will love receiving feedback from your actual users and contributors.

Pro Tip 1: Go to hackathons!

Hackathons are getting more popular and more frequently organized as they're a great way to bring people together. You're usually closed up with a few people to work on a project for a while, sometimes up to three or four days. By the end you'll have a team, a detailed concept, even a demo version of a product. Sounds good, doesn't it?

Pro Tip 2: Find a supportive workplace

At the company a friend of mine works for, they have an 'Experiment Day' every month. It's great for trying out interesting technologies. Similar ideas are found across a lot of tech companies—and it's easy to see why. You could even be the person who organizes these events.

I've heard that at some companies they have a "Demo Day" where anyone from the company can show what they've been working on in their free time.

There is also Google's famous "20% policy", which means their employees can work on anything they want for up to 20% of their work time. Why would a company do that? Because they've recognized that it's beneficial for their employees and their company too.

Keep in mind that if you create something using company time or computers, it may legally belong to your employer, so check your contract to make sure you're aware of that possibility.

So why not start one?

As you can see, your precious time spent working with side projects can be beneficial. Your small ideas can even grow into big companies. I hope that you are all motivated now to start and to finish one! In the end, the most important thing you can do is to grow and gain experience.

Getting your first job

Isaac Lyman with Clifford Fajardo

Getting hired is hard at first. I mean, eventually you'll have an amazing resume and recruiters will be flooding your inbox with interview requests, but for the first little while it can seem like an incredibly tough market. Everyone's looking for senior developers, interviews are all whiteboards and obscure data structures, and some jobs turn out to be unpaid "internships" or "software farms" that mistreat and devalue their employees.

Luckily, software development is a field where you can get a lot of valuable experience without even having a job. And there are things you can do to improve your resume, grow your network, build your skills, and interview at better companies, all without a heavy time investment.

Side projects

Coding in your spare time may not be appealing or even possible for everyone, but it's an effective way to add qualifications to your resume. Even a small project put together over the weekend can add value to your portfolio. There are a few different sites where you can upload your projects for free. The most popular[51] is GitHub[52], with over 100 million projects hosted, but BitBucket and GitLab are also popular choices.

A side project can fulfill many purposes. It can help you learn a framework or tool that's trending in the market, explore a technique you want to apply at work, exercise your creativity, prototype a product you want to start your own company with, and/or demonstrate your technical skills. And because you're building it for yourself, you may find that it's far less frustrating than coding at your day job. In fact, if my job is growing too tedious, I sometimes use a side project to remind myself why I love code. Taking time to create without limits or rules is always refreshing.

Potential employers who review your projects will be looking for a few different things:

- Well-organized folders and files. Most programming languages and frameworks have conventions for how things are organized. If your chosen technology doesn't, use a consistent structure that makes everything easy to find. Most files should be relatively small (a few hundred lines or less).
- Consistent code style. It doesn't matter what styles you choose (tabs or spaces, line lengths, brackets on their own line), as long as you stick to them.
- Unit tests. Writing tests shows that you care about code quality and maintainability.

[51]https://en.wikipedia.org/wiki/Comparison_of_source-code-hosting_facilities#Popularity
[52]https://github.com/

- Documentation. The ability to describe and explain your code makes you a better teammate. You should at least have a "Readme" file explaining how to set up the project and run the tests.

If you have trouble coming up with project ideas, start with something simple: a tic-tac-toe game, an "About Me" web page, a metric unit converter.

Revising your resume

When you're working on your resume, consider the following guidelines:

- Use standard, professional typefaces like Helvetica or Times New Roman. Don't use more than two.
- Use a professional-looking email address. Employers will think twice about interviewing you if your email address is "doomslayer420@onlinedating.com".
- Put the most impressive stuff at the top of your resume and the least impressive stuff at the bottom. If that means your education and job experience are on page 2, that's okay. Don't let fluff like a "personal statement" or "career goal" take the top spot unless it's expected in the industry or culture you're applying in.
- Don't overcomplicate. Unless you're a visual designer, you should avoid using images, illustrations, or multiple colors.
- People scan down the left side of the page when they're in a hurry, so left-align everything and put main points like categories, job titles, and project names in bold or capital letters.
- Be consistent. Make sure you're using the same typeface, font size, emphasis, bullets, alignment and spacing throughout your resume for headers and text at every level.
- Mention specific technologies, programming languages, and projects you've worked with. Hiring managers love specifics.
- Hiring managers also love numbers. Quantify your work wherever you can. Even if your last job was shift manager at a fast food place, you can say something like "Responsible for $2 million per year of physical product, serving over 180,000 customers."
- Resumes aren't only for job history. Include everything you've done that's relevant to your career. If you have a blog or GitHub profile, you've presented at a meetup or contributed to open source projects, you were president of a coding club in high school, or you were top of your class at development bootcamp, it belongs on your resume!
- Always provide your resume as a PDF.
- Don't call your resume "Resume.pdf". It will get lost too easily. Instead, use your name, job title, and (optionally) the date of the most recent revision: "Isaac Lyman - Software Engineer - Mar 2019.pdf".
- If English isn't your first language, ask a native speaker to review your resume and help you with spelling and grammar. This can make a big difference in the number of interviews you get.

A resume doesn't have to be complicated. Here's mine (slightly anonymized):

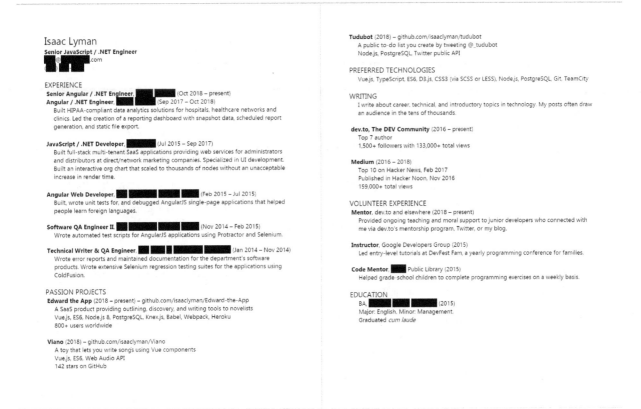

Meetups, events and channels

The best way to meet other developers and find out about jobs that aren't posted online is to go to meetups and events. Meetups are easily found in most cities, and often associated with a specific technology or product (for example, you can Google "Vue meetup" or "Adobe user group"). If you go to a small meetup, you may be asked to introduce yourself, which is a great opportunity to mention that you're looking for work. By the time the meetup is over you should have a couple of new leads. Larger meetups don't usually do this, but you can still meet a lot of local developers and find new opportunities if you attend.

Tech companies sometimes host events for developers to socialize and learn about their products, so this can also be a good way to expand your job search. You can find out about these events by following those companies and their employees on social media. (Programmers in particular have a strong presence on Twitter.) Tech conferences can be good events for networking as well, but are usually expensive (they assume your company is paying for the ticket).

It's also pretty common for a city—or, in the case of Utah, an entire state—to have a Slack workspace or other chat room for software developers. If you join, you can find out about open job opportunities by searching the archives or asking around. If you belong to a minority group, you can find a relevant

Slack channel (like latinos.slack.com[53] for Latinx people in tech, blacksintechnology.slack.com[54] for black people, or womenintechto.com[55] for people who identify as women, genderqueer or non-binary).

Learning about roles from other developers is ideal. They'll usually tell you more about a company's work environment, benefits, and pay than you'd learn from an online posting or a recruiter.

Mentors

A strong connection to someone with a lot of industry experience can be game-changing. If you don't have a mentor, set a goal now to find one. "Professional generosity" is one of the unwritten core values of the programming world, so if you reach out to a few developers you'll likely find at least one who's willing to answer questions, introduce you to recruiters, and give you career advice. (Others may be too busy or just not interested—don't let that discourage you.)

In your search for a mentor and in your career in general, social media can be invaluable. If you don't have an account on Twitter or LinkedIn, setting one up is a great next step. An account on dev.to[56] will also help you meet and learn from other programmers.

The best way to begin a mentoring relationship is to choose a programmer you know or admire, introduce yourself if they don't know you, and ask them a specific knowledge-based question, like "how did you find your first job?" or "can you help me understand how to search an array?" If they don't respond, you can follow up later, but don't be offended if they never get back to you (some programmers get hundreds of requests like this). If they do respond and the interaction goes well, you can ask another question or even ask for help with something bigger, like "can you help me practice for my next interview?" or "can you introduce me to someone in your area who's hiring?" Be patient and let the relationship grow. If you are polite and thank them for their time, you could end up with a connection that will transform your whole career.

Keep in mind that your mentor is just another developer and they don't know everything. They won't be able to solve all your problems or tell you exactly what to do. But their encouragement and advice can still make a big difference.

Interviewing

Interviewing is a skill that most people have to learn the hard way. The best way to get better at it is to practice; apply for a variety of jobs, even jobs you don't feel qualified for.

Companies vary widely by the way they vet candidates. Be prepared for multiple types of interviews:

- An *unstructured interview* is one of the most popular but least effective forms of screening. Any interview where the questions aren't chosen in advance is unstructured. These often

---

[53]http://latinos.slack.com/
[54]http://blacksintechnology.slack.com/
[55]http://womenintechto.com/
[56]https://dev.to

include questions about your work experience, hobbies, problem-solving approach, and career goals. I recently read a story about a CEO who hired someone on the spot after a brief, casual conversation, claiming that he could tell more about a person from five minutes face-to-face than from any amount of structured interviewing. This CEO was wrong. Multiple[57] studies[58] have[59] found[60] that selecting candidates using unstructured interviews is worse than choosing them at random.

- A *take-home project* is a technical assignment candidates are expected to complete on their own time, like creating a simple website or adding features to an example app. This usually takes four to five hours. Be aware that some companies use this as a dishonest way to get free work; if you're being asked to spend an unreasonable amount of time, or to do work that an employee would do, ask them to pay you for your time.
- A *verbal technical interview* is a structured interview including several questions about programming languages, technologies, software architecture, and problem-solving. Many companies make the mistake of asking questions that could easily be Googled on the job. You can prepare for these using a Google query such as "JavaScript interview questions".
- A *whiteboard interview* involves asking candidates to write code on a whiteboard without consulting reference books or the internet. Whiteboarding is quickly falling out of style because writing code on a board and writing code on the job are very different skills. If you are asked to whiteboard, focus more on finding a solution than writing perfect code. Even pseudocode (see Appendix A) is usually fine.
- A *live coding interview* is an interview where candidates are asked to write code while the interviewer watches, either in person or on a screen-sharing call. Being watched while you code can be nerve-wracking, but it's also something you can easily practice with a friend.
- A *short-term contract* is like a "trial period" for employment. Candidates sign a limited contract (usually for less than a month) during which they work like a regular employee and are paid by the hour. When the contract is complete, the candidate may be hired as a full-time employee.

In every contact with a company, remember that it's not about why you need *them*—it's about why they need *you*. Figure out what kinds of problems you're good at solving, then communicate that to them clearly and confidently.

Be sure not to let your interviews be one-sided. Take the opportunity to ask serious questions about the company. Some of my favorite things to ask in an interview are:

- "What keeps you at this company when there are so many other opportunities for a software developer like yourself?"
- "How much overtime have you worked in the last year?"
- "How hard is it to buy an educational book on company money?"

---

[57] http://journal.sjdm.org/12/121130a/jdm121130a.pdf
[58] https://blogg.hrsverige.nu/wp-content/uploads/2010/04/Stubborn1.pdf
[59] https://www.nytimes.com/2017/04/08/opinion/sunday/the-utter-uselessness-of-job-interviews.html
[60] https://hbr.org/2016/04/how-to-take-the-bias-out-of-interviews

Depending on the culture and circumstances where you live, you may also want to ask about company ethics, paid time off, parental leave, retirement savings plans, tuition reimbursement, or anything else that's important to you (for a longer list of values that might fit the bill, check out keyvalues.com[61]). This is stuff you don't want to be surprised by later on.

Keep in mind that some interview questions are illegal in many parts of the world. For example, in the United States, an interviewer cannot ask certain questions[62] about your marital or family status, sexual identity, disabilities, or religion, among other things.

It's worth checking the company's reviews on Glassdoor before the interview to look for red flags—every company will have a few negative reviews by former employees who had a bad experience or got fired, but if a lot of reviews talk about similar issues, that may be something to keep in mind or even ask about in your interview.

Negotiating

Getting your first job offer is exciting, but the process isn't over yet. Negotiation is an important opportunity to learn more about your value, the company's benefits, and what's important to them. There are five basic rules of negotiation:

1. *Always negotiate.* Every offer is negotiable, but most candidates are too nervous to stand up for themselves. Even if negotiating makes you anxious (like it does for me), the value is hard to ignore—an hour or so of negotiation can get you tens of thousands of dollars more. Some unfunded companies and nonprofits aren't willing to budge on salary; all the same, bringing it up will give you leverage to ask for other things you care about, like flexible hours, remote work options, vacation time, sick leave, parental leave, or stock options. And almost nobody will fault you for asking, even if they have to say no.

2. *Don't tell them how much you currently make.* This makes it too easy for them to offer you just a little bit more, instead of what they really think you're worth. If they ask, say "out of respect to my current employer and their policies, I can't share that information." Some places (like California, USA) even have laws prohibiting employers from asking.

3. *Take your time.* Don't let anyone rush you. If you start running out of steam in a negotiation, or just aren't getting the offer you want, say "that's a generous offer and I appreciate it, but I'm sure you understand this is a big decision and I need some time to think it over. I really hope we can figure out an offer that makes sense to both of us."

4. If they give you a salary number, say *"that offer is interesting; can you do better?"* (borrowed from Patrick McKenzie[63]). Really, that's all you have to say. Then quietly wait for them to respond. Count to 100 in your head if the silence grows uncomfortable.

5. If they ask you for a salary number, *tell them the highest number you can say without laughing* (borrowed from Cindy Gallop[64]). They may not meet that number, but they'll probably offer

[61]https://www.keyvalues.com/
[62]https://www.betterteam.com/illegal-interview-questions
[63]https://twitter.com/patio11/status/1046569259743100928
[64]https://www.bustle.com/articles/129373-how-to-get-a-raise-no-matter-what-according-to-businesswoman-cindy-gallop

you more than they would have otherwise—whether it be in salary, job title, flexibility, or other benefits. It helps if you've done some research already so you know what's reasonable for your job title and where you live—but whatever the salary range is, aim for the high end.

Negotiation is an uncomfortable and sometimes long process, but it can teach you a lot about the company you're applying to work with. And it can put you years ahead on salary increases and career progression.

Growing and succeeding

It may take you a while to get your first job offer, and that's okay. It doesn't mean you're a bad candidate. It doesn't mean you're in the wrong profession. Keep trying, keep interviewing, keep building your network. Good opportunities are out there.

My first job

Muhammad Arslan Aslam

My first job was at a small tech firm as a Junior Front End Developer. The salary was low, but I was desperately needy and eager to get into the industry, learn, and work. I didn't care about anything in the contract. They asked me when I could join, and I went straight to the office the very next day.

I learned a lot there about many things. Design. User experience. Development. WordPress. It was a good journey for a couple of months until they started asking me to stay late. I knew that on rare occasions, if a project was past the deadline or close to it, putting in some extra hours to complete it wasn't gonna hurt. But an extra 5-6 unpaid hours per day? That was a lot to ask for, considering I wasn't even getting paid as much as the average intern.

I left the company after one year and they never paid me my last month's salary.

A month later I got another job offer. This time I asked about company policies regarding overtime, medical expenses, staying late, etc.

It worked very well for a few months but then it was the same story all over again. The manager would force me to stay late and would even say he wasn't going to let me leave until I was finished. I'd get late night calls to get up and do something because the person who was responsible for it wasn't picking up the call. I would work from midnight until 8AM and couldn't be late for work afterward.

I actually blogged about it when I was getting frustrated with the situation and got a lot of feedback from the community, including senior developers, which helped me a lot. Right after I published that post and heard people's advice, I decided to quit the job. I stood up for myself and told my manager that putting in so many extra hours was affecting my personal life and I had started to get depressed.

It felt like a prison (not that I've been to prison, but still). You know how you can sit in your room watching Netflix all day and it doesn't bother you, but if someone *orders* you to sit in your room and watch Netflix all day, it becomes an awful chore.

I was worried at first about leaving the job. I was getting good money and the medical insurance was a good thing (more or less) but I gained the courage to leave the job and move on.

There are a lot of things that happened as a beginner that I feel a little ashamed to share. I should've stood up for myself right then but I didn't. I thought I might not get another job. But fortunately for me, everything worked out.

I have a stable job now which pays me well. The hours are flexible and the work environment is great. Learning opportunities are abundant plus I get to work with people who are much more experienced than I am and everyone here is eager to teach.

To summarize a few things that I learned from all of these experiences:

- When signing a contract at your first job (or any job as matter of fact), read it carefully. Ask about the company's policies regarding different aspects of normal everyday work. The ideal would be if you could get some legal advice on it. If that's not possible, just ask someone who has been through the same process, a friend or family member. Be careful about what you sign.
- Stand up for yourself when there's an issue. If you "let it pass this one time," it's gonna stick forever. I ignored my boss being abusive once and he continued being abusive for the rest of my time there. Don't let that happen to you.
- In the tech industry, occasionally putting in extra hours to meet deadlines isn't necessarily a big deal. People do it a lot, some times more than others. But make sure it's not because of someone's ego. I was asked to stay late because my boss "just felt like it". That's over the line. Never settle for this kind of behavior.
- Know your rights. Workplace toxicity can affect your personal life and mental health. Unfortunately, in many Asian countries, management doesn't pay much attention to this serious issue. If you're not feeling well, you can't work properly. Workplace toxicity comes in many different forms. If you feel like you are suffering harassment from a co-worker, a manager or anyone else, contact the people in charge. If they don't do anything about it, reach out to other organizations or the authorities. Someone else at your company might be facing the same issue. Stand up for yourself and others too.
- Last but not least, *know your worth, and never settle for less.*

I got my dream job. Now what?

Desi Rottman

When I started my first job in tech, it was as a support team member at a website builder geared toward musicians. My background made me ideal: years of retail and entertainment-industry customer service, HTML and CSS experience with an interest in web design, a music business degree, and the vocabulary to communicate with low-level tech users. I was pumped—a dream job that felt created just for me. I'd never considered that there was a company out there that married my disparate passions, let alone that I could land a job there.

In that position, I was doing a lot of intense troubleshooting for both clients and co-workers while getting comfortable with how the tech industry works and how companies are structured. It was a company with a QA department of one, and though I fell in love with troubleshooting and breaking things, we already had a great employee in that position. I didn't see myself having the opportunity to transition over. A small, awesome company means low turnover, so I didn't really give much thought to if there would be additional positions on the QA team to transition to eventually. But when our new CEO did some restructuring, she promoted the old QA guy to Project Manager, and behold—I had the opportunity to train for my (new) dream job!

Over the course of a career, your dream job can change and shift—and that's a good thing. As you work you'll learn more about the industry you're in and see more facets of it, discovering positions you never knew existed. In tech and dev, things are always changing. There's always something new to learn or a new startup being founded. That's another reason you might have to continually revisit and redefine your "dream job": new positions and new fields are often being created, so your eventual dream job might not even exist today, though your dream company might.

Advancing in your career also opens more opportunities—and once you start to stagnate, even the perfect job can stop feeling perfect. That's a good thing, but it can feel confusing to know how to keep growing and keep going. After all, wasn't this your ideal position? When this happens in technology, we have a unique opportunity to shape and design our dream jobs.

Even if you're not in a place to consider a transition right now, it's beneficial to look around and see what types of positions are open from time to time. Being aware of what else is out there and interests you is important to keep in mind. Being able to clearly recognize the next great fit when you see it can help stave off self-doubt, while staying prepared to apply when opportunities arise can combat impostor syndrome.

What else is out there?

A great way to start considering what your new "dream job" might be is to review open positions even before you're ready to leave your company or position. Not only does this give you an idea of ıew skills or education you can focus on, it can also put new jobs, industries or technologies ır radar. Specialties like Developer Relations and industries like the Internet of Things might not have even been on the map when you started your tech career. As these categories get more popular and more positions are being created, keeping abreast of what companies are looking for lets you tailor your experience to a new, growing industry.

Case Study: Accessibility Expert

The web has long been developed with mainly able-bodied users in mind. In recent years, accessible development and design have become hot topics and very important for many companies, but as a relatively new priority, many experienced developers weren't focused on it in the past. Lindsey Kopacz of Acquia Professional Services is an Accessibility Expert, and she also teaches others how to make their products more accessible.

Feeling unsure of where to start looking for other things that would interest you? Take a look around at your co-workers. Is your project manager always asking the other dev team members interesting questions about their projects? Is the support team consistently bringing up the same pain point about accessibility? If those kinds of things interest you, keep your eye on them. See if there's an issue you can help the support team fix, or a project you can shadow the PM on. Not only will that open your eyes to another facet of your company's work, it could be something to add to your new dream job resume.

Case Study: UX Engineering

UX Engineering is a relatively new position that many companies are hiring for. It blends principles of UX/UI design with front-end development, and can really appeal to developers who have a bent toward user experience. Emma Wedekind of LogMeIn blends her past experience in engineering at IBM with her interest in design (which she exhibits in her open source project, Coding Coach) to build accessible design systems and user interfaces.

How to start preparing

Starting where you are is a good place to prepare. Look at your current company again, and take a look at what your co-workers' backgrounds are. See if anyone in an interesting position is willing to meet with you for coffee, or even an informational interview. Connecting with someone who is already doing what might be your next dream job will help you learn the real nitty-gritty of their position. It's also likely to help your confidence—it's a fairly low-stakes networking opportunity with someone you already share some commonalities with, and that can end up being a boost when you do start going to interviews again.

Social media sites, particularly places like Twitter and StackOverflow, are also excellent places to learn about emerging tech, connect with others in the space, and even find open positions. The same principle applies here—if you see someone doing work that interests you, try to send them a DM and ask some questions about what they do and how they got there.

Keep your resume and portfolio up to date as you continue to learn and grow your skills, putting most of the focus on the tasks you hope to primarily work on in your next dream job. You'll thank yourself for this later when you don't have to try to throw something together at the last minute when the dream job gets posted.

As you continue to build your skills and learn more about technologies or areas you're drawn to, taking on a side project or signing up for a class to further your knowledge in that specialty will also help you get that much closer to the new dream job. If you're not sure what new skills to build, start looking at job descriptions for other positions that interest you. You'll get an idea of what employers are looking for in hires for that position, and you'll have some great experience and project examples to add to your portfolio!

> **Case Study: User Experience Advocate**
>
> I always knew that advocating for users and keeping our product looking and working well, while providing them the features they're looking for, was where my passion was. What I didn't realize was that this is an actual position that many companies are looking for! By doing research into what other types of opportunities are out there, it's allowing me to tailor my skills and experience so that when I am ready to leave (or get promoted), I'll be confident and ready.

More things to consider

As you start to think about what kind of work you might be interested in next, you'll likely start noticing some trends in the job postings. When you see another description that makes your heart soar, take a look at a few things:

- Job Title: Job titles may not say much about the actual position duties, especially in tech—"Rockstar Ninja" or "Smile Engineer" doesn't say very much about the day-to-day. Focus on the responsibilities listed rather than the hip titles.
- Education Requirements: Do they require a computer science degree, or a master's degree? Do they consider experience as an equivalent? If they do have a hard requirement for a degree, and it's not one you already have, consider if you're willing to get that degree or endorsement. (And if they aren't interested in applicants with diverse experience and education, that may be a red flag in itself.) Get in touch with someone who is already in that position and see if that's truly required for the kind of work you want, or if they use it as a screening funnel for applicants. Furthering education is understood as a requirement for advancement these days, and this can help you know where to focus to be ready for the next position.

Maybe the next move in your ideal career is less about the *kind* of work you're doing, and more about *where* you're doing it. It's becoming more and more common for "employment goals" to refer to a company rather than a specific position, and that could be something else to consider if you're looking to move on from that first dream job.

- Lifestyle: Another big consideration in sussing out your next dream job is the intangible quality-of-life factor. Maybe you've enjoyed being a full stack developer, but you're feeling maxed out on your career growth and want to make a transition to system administration. Is it worth making a nice six-figure salary if you're required to be on-call 24/7 to fix any issues? Are you willing to sacrifice a big-city salary in order to have a remote position? These are more ethereal issues that aren't going to be nicely laid out in a job posting, so being prepared to know what you will or won't accept from a company can well prepare you.

One last (but no less important) facet to consider here is the culture of a prospective new company. Similar to the lifestyle you'll have, think about what's important to you at work—a kitted-out game room with arcade games and ping pong tables, with weekly happy hours in the break room, but the understanding that you work closer to 50 hours a week? Or would you rather have less fancy "perks," but more flexibility and freedom? Do the employees seem to relish being there beyond 9-5 hours? In an effort to promote diversity and reduce harassment or abuse, codes of conduct are growing in popularity. Does this company have one that reinforces the culture you want to associate with? Another common "perk" for companies is providing philanthropic opportunities—paid days off for volunteering, or matching employee donations to nonprofits. If possible, try connecting with someone at the company you're interested in to get some of your questions about these things answered.

Does that company culture align with your values? If not, maybe it's not actually your dream company. If the company's ethics don't align with your own, you might not be taking pride in your work, which can take a toll mentally.

Keeping these things in mind is important for any job change in your career, but it can also help you really develop your dream job description.

Exercise

To start evaluating your next move, even if it feels far off, try to take a look every week or two at open positions at your dream company. If you see one that particularly interests you, save it to your computer. Highlight or circle aspects of the job that interest you, and you can update your resume or portfolio using the same wording.

This also helps you to know what parts of the job you wouldn't be interested in—your "dream job" likely has parts that feel very dry to you, and that's important to keep in mind as you continue searching as well.

Keeping up to date and being educated on other current openings and industry growth will make you confident that you'll know when your new dream job pops up, and be ready to land it!

Burnout, part 1

James Turner

Editor's Note: Burnout is so pervasive and harmful in tech that I've chosen to include two perspectives on it. Programmers burn out for a lot of different reasons and you will either witness it or experience it yourself at some point. When that happens, take some advice from these authors and make a change.

You may have heard the phrase "burnout" before. I can assure you that in this context it has nothing to do with cars laying down rubber.

Occupational burnout is a feeling of exhaustion, where what you previously enjoyed working on becomes less enjoyable, where things get on your nerves more easily or even where you have feelings of depression. One of the first uses of the phrase dates back as far back as 1974 when psychologist Herbert Freudenberger used the term in one of his published works.

At the end of 2014, I had the opportunity to take on more responsibilities where I worked, being promoted from a Web Developer to an Account Manager. While I was still programming, my new responsibilities included liaising with clients, discussing business requirements as well as managing current and upcoming projects. It was a great experience and I am grateful to have had that opportunity, but it wasn't without its problems.

I may not have been the "cool" or "fun" person in the office, but I'd say I was the "brains trust"—there wasn't a problem I wouldn't try to help solve and most of the time I was successful. I may not have even known anything about the topic beforehand but if someone asked me a question, I would as quickly as possible research the topic to work out the answer. This eagerness to help my colleagues, while an admirable trait, was one part of my problem. It took time to be thorough and I didn't want my colleagues to struggle on something that I could help them with.

I didn't just want to avoid disappointing my colleagues, I didn't want to disappoint my boss—I had been given this great opportunity and trusted to do it well. I am a good programmer, and one day I'd like to think I'll be a good boss, but some of the traits that make me a good developer didn't transfer as well to this role as I hoped. Larger projects were coming in on top of the business-as-usual work which led to work piling up. I was in meetings every other day, constantly liaising with clients and managing projects while also still programming. Rather than tell anyone that I was struggling, I decided I'd just work a few extra hours that week to make sure everything was done. Those few extra hours in a week turned into a few extra hours each day till it even got as bad as working an additional day on top of those extra hours.

While no one asked me to do those extra hours and I didn't even want to do them, I still did them because I believed it was just a short-term thing that would blow over soon. I was tired, I was stressed, and every morning I didn't even want to go to work yet the problems that led me here were so simple.

In mid-2015 the stress peaked and my colleagues were starting to take notice. Two of my colleagues took me out to lunch to see how I was doing. They asked me if I was okay, knowing something was going on, and I said no, I wanted to quit. I talked through what was happening with them, they understood the issues and were sympathetic. They gave suggestions on how to make my workload easier, helping me with anything I needed. Over the next few months, things were a little easier and I stopped pushing myself as hard to please everyone.

It took just over 6 months to go from an employee happy to come to work to one who dreaded it because I couldn't stand the thought of disappointing others. It took a single lunch out for me to admit how far I had gone and start the journey back to a happier me.

Identifying burnout from the point of view of the person experiencing it is hard—how do you know if the stress you're feeling about a situation is burnout or not? Burnout, however, isn't black and white; it is many shades of grey. Burnout may reach a tipping point but that is not a useful measure to help prevent burnout in the future. With how the feelings of burnout can gradually build up, you need to look at your own long-term trends in your life. From your mood, to sleep patterns, to diet, to participation in social gatherings—these can all help indicate whether something is changing in your life.

One of the more obvious indicators for me should have been realising that I didn't want to go to work when I woke up in the morning. While this feeling might happen for a lot of different reasons, it is an indication that something is up in your life and it is best to evaluate what that might be.

Determining the cause for such feelings is incredibly important in trying to address them. When trying to identify the cause, it is best to keep an open-minded approach as it really can be from things you didn't even realise. The causes that lead to burnout don't even need to be exclusive to your job, they can be events in your personal life or social circles.

The causes leading to my burnout came from my actions at my job, not from my personal life and not from expectations by my colleagues or boss. I chose to accept the opportunity to take on more responsibilities and I chose to work extra hard to make sure I would succeed. This may seem like I am trying to carry the burden for the situation, but I don't blame myself for burning out. Instead, I take responsibility for the fact that my own actions allowed stress to build up.

Although I can say that about my situation, it doesn't necessarily mean that your feelings of burnout are caused by you. You may not be remotely the cause of the feelings; you are only responsible for how you handle those feelings and what you are going to do about them.

The most appropriate action for handling burnout will vary widely depending on the cause. With that being said, the one thing you can always do to help your state of mind is to talk to someone about the situation. It may be best that this person is not involved in what you believe are the causes, but the key here is that you are talking about it at all. The reason I see this being effective is the same reason Rubber Duck Debugging (see Appendix A, "Rubber Ducking") is effective: when you talk through a problem aloud it can help you have a deeper understanding of it, leading to ways to resolve it.

When you are on the path to resolving your feelings of burnout, I think it is important to consider what you want your future self to be. Of course you want to be happy and healthy but is it at the same job? Are you wanting to stay in this industry? Do you see yourself living in the same location or having the same friends? These questions might seem dramatic, but dramatic changes might be what you need. The decisions you make here are wholly your own and it is important to weigh everything in perspective to your own life.

If your causes are primarily job-related, it might be enough to try and move to a different team or department. For situations where you see no resolution at your workplace, speaking with your feet and finding a different job is the most powerful action. If your causes are primarily social life related, work out what specific things you could do to have a positive impact. Maybe at the end of the day, you may only need a break to do something else—only you will know if that is what is best for you.

When you have resolved your current feelings of burnout, it is important to stay vigilant as they can always creep back. Look after yourself; you only live once.

What if you're not the person experiencing burnout, but you want to make sure anyone you know or work with isn't having issues? While you can potentially identify it through a decrease in work performance or long-term changes in mood, it can be as simple as asking if they are okay. I wouldn't recommend doing it over a Slack message or in front of a group of people but if you can have a one-on-one conversation with them, don't hesitate to ask. Asking someone that question may be exactly what they are needing to hear, genuine support from a friend or colleague so they can evaluate themselves and their situation.

At the end of the day, while burnout can be a serious topic, it isn't an impossible problem to resolve and isn't something you need to handle alone.

Burnout, part 2

John Woodruff

Burnout: a hazard that the software industry is particularly prone to, and one that occurs far more often than it should. Over the course of your career you'll hear the stories of your co-worker's friend who burned out so badly they ended up changing careers. Perhaps it is closer to home and happens to someone you personally know. We all tell ourselves that it won't happen to us, that we love programming far too much to burn out, so we don't take the necessary steps to avoid it. But burnout is a very real threat, and it will happen to some extent to many of us. I didn't believe it could affect me, yet I have dealt with episodes of burnout throughout my career. By understanding burnout, its symptoms and causes, we can take concrete steps to avoid it altogether and to come back from being burned out.

Burnout is a slow process. You don't just wake up one day and suddenly you're burned out. For me it was a state that set in gradually, with the symptoms becoming worse over time. At the beginning, they may be insignificant enough that you barely notice anything is amiss, which makes it difficult to determine that you're on the path to burning out. There are a variety of symptoms that may manifest themselves. Please note that this is by no means an exhaustive list, these are simply some of the most common issues related to burnout.

You may feel *anxiety*, often about your job, usually carrying over into your personal life. It's also common to experience *depression*, especially if you are already prone to it, but someone who has never felt depressed before can experience it as a symptom of burnout. One of the most common symptoms is a *lack of attention span and motivation* at your place of work. It becomes very *difficult to focus* on tasks, in meetings, and during general workplace activities. You may feel constantly exhausted, both at work and at home, whether or not you've gotten enough sleep. It can affect your sleep too, possibly manifesting itself in new or worsening *insomnia*. You may find yourself becoming more *irritable* or *pessimistic* in your interactions with friends and co-workers. You could experience *guilt* for not feeling like you used to in your job, or like you perceive your co-workers feel.

All of this and more leads to the most common symptom: *poor job performance*. You are no longer motivated to do your work. Tasks that once would have seemed small to you suddenly appear enormous or insurmountable. You may find yourself coming in late, taking extra long breaks, or leaving early because you feel like you can't handle it. You aren't paying attention or participating in meetings where your input is wanted or required, which affects everyone involved. Unchecked burnout can even lead to the need to stop programming altogether and change careers. Sadly, it's happened to many people before and it will continue to happen unless we as developers take the proper steps to recover from and avoid burnout.

To understand how to avoid burnout, we need to first understand the common causes. There are many reasons and ways one might get burned out. The most common ways are usually directly related to long term stress without relief. This could include any number of scenarios, including working long hours for too long without a vacation; constantly working on projects that have unrealistic deadlines set by others without your input; being stuck on project maintenance while you watch other developers working with cool new tools and technologies; having an unhealthy work-life balance that is skewed too far towards work; or working in a dysfunctional environment that makes you feel unsafe. All of these contribute directly to your level of burnout.

I've experienced many of those scenarios, and unless you're exceptionally lucky, you will too throughout your career. My most recent episode of burnout was due to being on a project for two years with no end in sight—a project I desperately wanted to succeed, but which seemingly had everything thrown in its way to stop it from doing so. The stresses of that environment grew and grew until I found myself dreading going to work. I couldn't fall asleep at night for hours thinking about this project. I no longer wanted to work on the previously enjoyable side projects I'd had going on. In addition to that, the project was frequently put on hold for another project that had an extremely short deadline imposed by others that I had no control over. So instead of finishing the new project and being relieved to go back to my old project, it was simply more stress. It was a very difficult time in my career.

The above situation boils down to several basic feelings you might relate to. You feel *stuck* or *trapped* with no end in sight. You are dealing with *impossible goals* which makes you more depressed each time you miss them. You've *overworked* yourself. When the mind has endured high levels of stress for too long, it becomes exhausted and craves relief. This *exhaustion* is central to many of the symptoms I listed previously, such as anxiety, depression, and lack of focus. If you let any of this get too far without intervention, you risk burning yourself completely out of your career.

With all that in mind, let's talk about avoiding burnout. If you're currently suffering from burnout, these principles apply to recovering from burnout as much as to avoiding it. In short, it's about taking control of your professional (and personal) life, which will help you to be a well-balanced individual. Having proper balance in our lives leads to better mental and physical health, improved mood and happiness, and increased productivity, whether that be at work or in other pursuits.

The first thing you need to do is make sure you *set proper boundaries.* You're in a form of a relationship with your work and employer, and as with any other type of relationship, good boundaries exist to keep the relationship healthy and happy. While looking for a job, you should know the limits of what you're able and willing to do for the company. An employer may have the expectation that you work 12 hour days, 6 days a week (rather than a standard 40 hour week) to further the goals of the company. They may think you should forego using your vacation time to put in more hours at work. While there may be people who are okay with that kind of an environment, I see it as a form of abusive relationship between employer and employee. With the companies I've worked for thus far, I've been very careful to research their culture and determine whether I would be required to do things that are unreasonable and go past my established boundaries. This is not to say, of course, that I refuse to work a minute past 40 hours. There have been many occasions where I've worked long hours to meet a deadline, fix an issue, or help mentor someone else. In these situations, however, I was usually able to recover adequately by (for example) taking a day off the next week.

The ability to *take time off* is key to avoiding burnout. Time off, even if that's simply making sure you don't work on the weekend, is time our mind needs to be able to recover from the stresses of the workplace. By working constantly with little to no breaks, that mental stress continues to build without relief, slowly burning you out. It's a common false belief that by working that much, you'll become a better programmer. I held that belief at the beginning of my career and have since changed my attitude. In the long run, becoming burned out will severely harm, if not destroy, your ability to work effectively. Taking a vacation where you completely disconnect from work (and coding in particular) can be incredibly therapeutic for programmers who may be slowly burning out. Even doing this during the weekends can help stave off the struggles that are associated with burnout, so make sure to take the time for yourself to unplug and rejuvenate. Also take advantage of your employer-provided vacation days; they're given specifically as a benefit for you to use to recharge.

There are many other small things I recommend for helping to keep your work-life balance in check. Engaging in non-work related hobbies and activities, for example, is a great way to keep your personal life separate from your work life. Keeping your body healthy through regular exercise is also important and helps keep your mind stimulated. Perhaps the most helpful thing to do is to be consistent. Inconsistency causes stress, and if there's anything we've learned thus far, it's to reduce the amount of stress we feel on a regular basis.

Occasionally more drastic measures are necessary. While most of my small burnout episodes were solved by taking a couple days or a week off from work and totally disconnecting to rejuvenate, the most recent episode I talked about required a different approach when my standard methods had failed. It wasn't so bad that I quit coding, but it was bad enough that I was no longer in an environment conducive to a good career. I needed to find a new job and get out of that situation so I could bring myself back. I'm very happy to report that at the time of writing I'm happily employed at a new company working on a product that is much more stable and healthy than what I was on previously. I also am part of an excellent team that highly values work-life balance and shows it by example. I've never been happier in my career than I am right now, mere months after dreading going in to work.

Burnout is a difficult trial to overcome, but if I can tell you anything, it's that it can be recovered from successfully. I can say that from experience, having felt varying levels of burnout at various times throughout my career. Even better than recovering from burnout is avoiding it entirely, something I've re-committed myself to more fully in recent months. By putting into practice the recommendations mentioned above and taking control of our professional lives, we can make real strides towards keeping our personal and work life in balance, and keeping burnout at bay.

Do I fit in?

Editor's Note: Following are some true stories and advice from developers who have wondered if tech is the right place for them. If you've had the same doubts, I hope their words will encourage you.

Sabrina's story

Sabrina Gannon

Despite coming from what's generally considered a traditional computer science background, "Do I fit in?" is a question I've had to tackle many times in my programming career. The first time I asked myself this question was when I was applying to university for Computer Science, because math was the subject I performed lowest in and English was my highest. The most exposure I had to code came in the form of customizing my Neopets HTML pages; it was just enough to make me curious enough to take the leap and apply anyway.

I thought a University degree would give me a feeling of legitimacy that would put the nagging question "Do I fit in?" to a stop. Instead, the work I did at a very research-focused University, alongside many classmates who had far more coding experience than I did, exacerbated the feeling to the point that I doubted I would even finish my degree, let alone have a sunny employment outlook.

My first technical full-time role came in the form of an internship the summer after I'd finished my degree; this was the next level of questioning my own sense of belonging and identity. I had moved out of my family's home and across the country, and I was surrounded by smart people and learning about web development, a development specialization I had little to no experience in. It was a whirlwind, and I spent far too much time convinced that my presence there was happenstance.

At the end of that internship, a full time job offer came through. My four month interview had paid off, and what felt surreal became that much more so. This is a moment I come back to often on the more difficult "Do I fit in?" days, because that was one day that I can look to as a source of validation. I definitely recommend collecting these moments to remind yourself when the little voice suggesting you don't belong speaks up, because there will always be moments when it does and being prepared to tell it off never hurts.

Being a woman does not help with managing this feeling; being reminded how rare you are because of your gender in a group project does nothing positive for feelings of imposter syndrome. Nor does the implication that you might get hired to inflate a company's diversity numbers and be a spokesperson for them. These were all said to me casually, as if they were stating the sky is blue, which made them that much easier to internalize.

There will be jerks, and worse, there will be jerks who aren't even self-aware enough to be called jerks.

But in all these steps, I met good people too. People who encouraged me to take a chance on myself when I otherwise would have backed down, people who listened to me unpack the self doubt and negative thoughts that I'd internalized along the way. Without them, I wouldn't have had the opportunity to take the next step. I've been very fortunate to know them, and now am very fortunate to be able to be this person for others as well.

Here's what I've learned time and time again when I'm faced with the question "Do I fit in?":

- A lot of what made me feel excluded was rooted in technical jargon I didn't know and the fact that everyone using it seemed so much smarter than me.
- Tech is a huge, vast field—no one knows everything, and adaptability is key. Taking the time to figure out how I learn best and continually invest in that development has helped me offset my experiences with imposter syndrome immensely.
- Be patient with yourself!
- Take note of and celebrate little wins and steps forward.
- Keep an ear to the ground on what's going on in the industry, the types of conversations being had. I find Twitter useful for this.
- There are jerks, but there are also good people out there. Don't be afraid of seeking them out; whether through local meetups or online communities, growing your support network really helps you foster a sense of belonging for yourself and others.
- If you are coming from a non traditional background, that is an asset; don't let anyone convince you otherwise. Many of the skills that make me most effective at working with others and communicating with stakeholders were gained working part-time jobs while I was in school.

My own answer to the question "Do I fit in?" is always shifting. I've found the more that you work and engage with others to make a given environment a little warmer and more welcoming, the more you'll find yourself a place to fit into that process, and while tech might have a few characters who seem resistant to this, every day there are more and more people like you—people who have wondered if they fit in—writing their first line of code.

My software developer journey

Clifford Fajardo

At the beginning of 2016, I had just graduated from a coding boot camp, finished a long job search and was starting my career as a software developer at Salesforce in San Francisco. I was excited about the journey ahead and equally very nervous.

I felt as if I had stepped into a whole new world! I was starting my first full-time job; I was now working in a corporate environment; I was working on a fully remote team; I was worried that I didn't fit the typical software developer profile and was concerned about how I would perform on the job.

This new world I had stepped into felt like a long shot from where I had come from. Before this job, I had been a student at community college and the only work experience I had at the time was as a student tour guide and pizza chef.

It was still hard for me to believe that I, a kid from a first generation immigrant family from Nicaragua who had been living on the poverty line for most of his life, was now the first person in his family to work in a corporate environment and the first to become a software developer.

As I transitioned into that role, it felt like I was on a roller coaster ride. There were lots of great high moments and low moments. I would have work days where I would create something or fix a bug and feel complete joy. There were other days where I questioned if this was the right career for me because of how challenging it felt or how long it was taking me to complete my work, relative to my peers.

There was even a point during my first year as a developer when I seriously questioned whether I fit in and belonged in this industry. I almost decided to go back to my old, easier but less fulfilling life, which for me meant not confronting my fears head on and growing from them.

When I had these types of days what helped me push through were the thoughts of my family and the vision I had when I first started to learn to code. The vision that one day I would become knowledgeable enough to build out any idea I could envision and impact the lives of millions of people.

Looking back, I'm so happy I didn't give in to my fears. If I had, I wouldn't have had the opportunity to later work at LinkedIn, my second job, where I worked on apps impacting over half a billion people. I would have missed out on the opportunity to gain the experience, knowledge, and confidence that I needed to eventually venture out and start working full time on the business and app I work on today.

Everyone is different, own your individuality

In retrospect, most of the low experiences and feelings I had about not belonging came from not appropriately managing my own expectations, my lack of experience, oftentimes my impatience, and being too hard on myself.

During tough times, it was easy to forget the reality of the situation I was in:

- I'm new to this job and industry, so it absolutely takes time to adjust.
- I'm taking longer than all my peers to complete tasks, but that's normal at any new job or role.
- Just like me, everyone on my team was once new and inexperienced at something.

And equally as easy to forget the things I had control over:

- Though I'm not at the level I want to be at now, I can make a change and take ownership of my learning and growth. It may require some extra time outside of work, but it's doable.
- I don't have to be the same person I was yesterday. I can learn to be a more effective leader, communicator, and developer. Pushing myself out of my comfort zone little by little every day will build my character and confidence.

- I don't have to travel on my journey alone. I can find a mentor or employee resource group and accelerate my learning and growth with the help of others.

Once I started realizing all of these things, all areas of my life quickly and dramatically improved. I no longer spent time thinking about whether or not I fit in, regardless of where I was. I finally internalized that I could carve out my own unique place, co-exist with everyone around me, and bring a different perspective to the table.

Own your unique experiences. Own your individuality and be open-minded. Be ready to learn, unlearn and relearn. Lastly, don't be too hard on yourself.

LGBT

Connor Ocampo

Do you identify as an LGBT person? Are you in the process of applying for jobs? Are you concerned with how you might fit in and want some tips on how to best go about including this information in your application? If yes, then this section is for you.

There are many reasons why someone may want to include these personal details in their application, the most important one being to avoid employment with a company that discriminates. The fact is, discrimination among all kinds of minority groups is still a very real occurrence. Because of this, it's important to safeguard yourself against any potential threat that may happen, be it physical, mental or emotional.

Everyone wants to work for a company where they are accepted and can work comfortably. The good news is, there are steps we can take to ensure this outcome.

In this section, I'll outline what I did to communicate my gender identity and other possible ways to go about including this information. I'll share with you how I went about arranging my portfolio to "wave the flag" and express my gender identity.

What I did to be visible

The first question I asked myself was, "how can I go about this while staying relevant to the application?" There were a couple steps I took to achieve this.

The first was to include one of my trans-related side projects in my portfolio—it was an online transgender and allied apparel company. In 2016, I found myself with a unique opportunity to create something, launch it, and see how the market responded. It was a success, I learned a lot, and I figured it was as good a project (and as relevant) as any to showcase in my portfolio.

This checked off two relevance requirements, one being that it was something I created, and two, it dealt with supporting transgender folks.

Now, I can't tell you how every recruiter felt about this information, but I can tell you that the subject of starting a company itself was a strong and positive talking point. And while I did worry that being so visible might hurt my job prospects, I reasoned with it by telling myself if they didn't accept it, then I'm better off not being in that environment.

If someone reading this was worried about "waving the flag", I'd tell them the same thing. Be strong in your conviction to be yourself. Be unapologetic about it! Anywhere with anyone that stands to discriminate against you isn't a place you want to be. And on a positive note, anywhere with anyone that stands to accept you and welcome you as you are is exactly the place you want to be!

Leaving more clues

Another approach I took was including personal details in my about/bio section of my portfolio website. These are more simple and subtle steps you can take to ensure that the company is aware of your identity.

I'm very transparent in mine, openly addressing my gender identity and my belief that it's important for minority groups to be visible. This is a great and appropriate way to be visible!

Visibility over 9000!

If you want to raise your visibility beyond those two methods, leave more digital footprints. Blog about LGBT topics that matter to you. These could be published on any digital medium, including your own personal website or on social media in microblog form. Just remember to include links to your social media profiles in your portfolio website if you choose to be visible on them!

If the hiring manager is thorough with vetting their candidates, these thoughtfully sprinkled-in details will surely catch their eye. And if they're a super awesome, diversity-advocating company, they'll have all the more reason to welcome you with open arms.

During the initial interview

First, congrats on the interview! You've done great so far. Time to keep going!

At this stage in the interview process, the conversation should be fairly laid back with the recruiter's focus being to get acquainted with you. In my experience, you'll find a lot of opportunities to speak about what you've worked on and what you're proud of so far. The recruiter usually sets the stage for this.

Ideally, it'd be a good idea to bring up two or three pieces of work with either an LGBT project or blog being casually looped in the mix. That way, if for whatever reason the recruiter overlooked that detail in your portfolio, it'd be 100% clear and open now for you to assess how they respond to it.

If they respond negatively, you'll know. I've never had this happen to me. But in case it does, stay cool, be the bigger person, and exit the conversation. We can flip this unfortunate situation and think of it as being one step closer to the right fit. The important thing here is to keep moving.

If they respond positively, you'll know. This has happened 100% of the time for me. In this case, stay cool (while having an internal celebration) and keep the conversation flowing. You'll feel great knowing that you were brave enough to bring it up and you'll be more comfortable and confident in the conversation.

Wrapping it up

The question of "Do I fit it?" can be a tough question to face, especially for individuals in historically oppressed minority groups. But take solace in knowing that times have changed and are continuing to change. We've come a long way as a society and you have the opportunity to allow it to keep going just by being open about who you are.

You are a smart, capable, and highly skilled human being deserving of respect. Whether you're lesbian, gay, bisexual, or transgender, being visible is important in your journey to fitting in with the right team.

I hope this section was able to help you in some way.

Best of luck to you, friend!

P.S. If you want to find an LGBT person like you in the tech industry, I'd search on social media (Twitter and Instagram). There are a lot of advocates present on social media. Of course, you're always welcome to send me a message as well. Here are my social channels: Twitter[65], Instagram[66], and LinkedIn[67].

---

[65] https://twitter.com/connorocampo
[66] https://www.instagram.com/connor_ocampo/
[67] https://www.linkedin.com/in/connorocampo/

Women in code

Ilona Codes

Introduction

I got my first PC when I was 11 years old and it became everything to me. I remember that "after computer" time when the real world didn't seem as interesting anymore. Like many children, I started spending hours playing video games, and with an internet connection, I went deeper into the flow of information and ideas.

As the years went by my interest in computers and computer science only increased. This played the main role in my career choice and selection of my university major. I was facing a choice between computer science and medicine. I couldn't decide what was more interesting to me. And as you've guessed by now, I made the decision to pursue computer science.

Early in my career I remember thinking, "maybe this was a bad decision." I tried to give up twice in my first year in the IT industry. There were many reasons and people around me at the time that made me strongly consider that. And I'm far from the only one who tried to quit the industry.

So, why do women turn away from technology careers?

Because there are spoken and unspoken barriers that make it difficult for women to advance in IT.

Talking to women in tech and code at different events, I've observed some common problems which have forced women to leave engineering careers:

- Poor working conditions: too much travel, lack of advancement, low salary, etc.
- Lack of respect for women in male-dominated fields.
- Unhealthy workplace climate: closed-minded managers, dev teams that are difficult to work with, or lousy company culture.

To boil it down to the most universal problem, we see that *bias* pushes women out of the industry. Moreover, that bias can play out even worse depending on a woman's race or ethnicity.

Nowadays coding is becoming one of the most in-demand skills across industries, and the milestones I'll discuss here will help you to "overcome" your first year in code if you are a woman. Because, honestly, being a software engineer is one of the best jobs for women. We implement products and make life easier for people who use them. Sometimes I feel like a hero doing it. Isn't that amazing?

But because of that *bias*, you can miss out on all the benefits of a programming career. Here's a list of the advantages of being a software engineer at the company where I currently work:

- We work five days a week. We have a flexible schedule and can even work from home.
- We learn new things constantly while solving problems, working with other software engineers, watching webinars, doing courses, visiting conferences, etc.
- We celebrate all occasions with our teams. We go to team parties and do team-building exercises.
- We make friends from different countries and cultures, and they enrich our life experience.
- We can easily switch from client to client or product to product. If we don't find our work challenging, we can change the type of work that we do.

It's not my first job, but so far it is my best one.

Choosing a company with the right values

Only now do I understand that when I was looking for my first job and sent out lots of applications for entry-level frontend positions, I didn't pay enough attention to the companies I was applying to.

I didn't even clearly understand the differences between types of companies: a startup? A consultancy? An agency? A public company? A product company?

I knew HTML, CSS, and JavaScript. And I had made fancy web pages and implemented mini projects to consolidate my technology stack knowledge and create a portfolio. My only focus was on getting professional experience—and finding my first job.

As a result, out of 20-30 CVs sent to different companies, I got 2-3 invitations to interviews. I didn't much care about what kind of company they were with, what products/services the company provided, the company's values or the team lead/manager I was going to work with. And that was a big mistake on my part. If I had known better, my first job could have been at a company I'd be happy to work at.

You can always get insights about a company before applying for a position. For example, through the company's reviews on job search websites. You can meet current and former employees at meetups or other events and get more details about the company's purpose or vision or whether the company has open positions at the moment.

Then Google the name of the company and check their job postings. After getting enough information, you can understand whether the company is diversity-friendly and worth applying at, how the company is organized, what the working process would be like for you there, etc.

Different types of software engineering jobs demand different kinds of preparation. If you've done your research and decided which company you would like to join, then start by sharpening your skills and focusing on your strengths and weaknesses. Do some side projects to learn the required tech stack for the position. Add all these to your resume and send it to the company.

If it's your first year in code, I would suggest you apply at startups and mid-size companies. These companies are full of hands-on work. You'll get good exposure to things to learn and, more importantly, your ideas and suggestions will be taken into consideration. You'll be able to challenge yourself, showcase your creativity and learn how to work on a team. These jobs can give you a clearer picture of yourself regarding what skills and knowledge you need to get. Also, you'll get the chance to build your professional network.

The importance of telling the truth

As women in tech, we always face more problems at work than men. This observation comes not only from my life experience but also from my women friends and acquaintances who work in IT. I am lucky now to be working in a healthy environment, and along with a professional relationship with management, we are building trust between the two sides: employer and employee.

Once, when I was visiting a meetup for women who code, I met Clara (name has been changed). She is a junior software engineer at company X.

At that time she was a new employee. And you know how it's difficult to adapt to company processes, a new project, and your coworkers in your first weeks or even months, especially if it's your first year in the field.

Later I texted her to invite her to meet up for a cup of coffee. I wanted to hear her story. While we were sitting in the cafe, drinking coffee and speaking about our jobs, Clara confessed that she was afraid of saying "I don't know" when in fact she didn't know something. Instead of that, she was trying to bluff her way through the situation and not lose control.

Her apparent reason was fear of looking stupid in front of her colleagues and managers at work. She's a competent professional and she must have an answer because it's her job, isn't it?

A year ago, I would have answered "Yes." It is my job. And I must know the answer to any question related to my expertise. But not now.

It took years for me to understand that when you are telling the truth, you can breathe easier. It's a straightforward and selfish reason, one I truly learned through my experience. There are many pros to the truth: you don't need to focus on backstories, and backstories of backstories, and relevant details to make what you're saying appear plausible, and making your body language match up with what you are saying.

When you are telling the truth, you are at peace; you are honest. So much less energy needs to be spent.

Don't be afraid of telling your team or manager that you cannot finish your work on time. I'm sure you had reasons, perhaps a specific problem or blocker. The best solution is to provide an explanation and make your case as to why you couldn't finish this task as planned.

If you are blocked by a problem and cannot find a workaround, don't hesitate to ask for help. An answer or some useful advice from a colleague or team member can easily unblock you and allow you to continue solving your problem. And it will help you solve the same problem in the future if it arises again.

In the end, you will only benefit from gaining new knowledge, learning how to work as a team, and spending less time on figuring out a solution.

Some people think that having a gap in knowledge is a weakness. But the real weakness is being close-minded and dishonest.

How to grow a thick skin and handle complexities

During my university studies I noticed that most of the students were men. Even at that time I could imagine how my future working environment would look. And I was right.

During my first year in code I worked with men as the only woman on my team, and to be honest, at that startup, it was hard to work together, not just for me but also for my teammates.

There was that bias against accepting code produced by me—by a woman.

Yes, women are different from men. And yes, women can definitely code. But many have stopped coding because someone once made them feel like they can't code *well*.

Looking back on that time, maybe you're a beginner without any practical working experience at all, still confused about processes, teamwork and code bases with tens or hundreds of thousands of lines of code. The combination of unknown things, complexity, and a new team where you're only an intern surrounded by middle-level/senior software developers—it can make you feel as though there's a massive amount of pressure on you.

In the beginning, it was a significant challenge to go to work. But I did it, even if I was crying. I understood the importance of it. I was trying to see things positively and benefit from them by:

- Learning from my failures
- Distinguishing between personal and business
- Trying to get constructive feedback from the team
- Not complaining about things

For the time being I worked with men, learned from them, and built stamina. And I saw how easily some men separate personal and business. They can be fighting with each other about a topic at work and then behave as if nothing happened. It's just work, nothing personal.

If you are in your first year in code, one of the first, most important things you have to do is start to develop a thick skin.

That means you have to be able to go into work, even if your performance isn't perfect, even if sometimes you don't completely understand what you are doing (or if you thought you did but in the end everything went wrong). At the same time, don't forget to appreciate yourself and your progress (which may be noticeable only to you), regardless of what happens.

Here are three more ideas for women on developing a thick skin:

1. Cut down your contact with abusive people

If your direct manager or team members are just plain unbearable and always trying to bring you down with their obsessive words or actions, then start looking to join a different team or switch jobs. You won't be able to stand this atmosphere for long and it can ruin your self-esteem and confidence.

2. Don't let harsh words hurt you

Sometimes we care too much about what others think.

This especially happens if you are the only woman on a team and worry about the image you are portraying to others. If someone insults you or insists on something you completely disagree with, it keeps repeating in your head over and over because we're taught to deal with that stuff head-on.

The best way to handle this situation is to replace the thought with a more positive one. Why should someone's negative words ruin your day?

Focus on yourself in this situation. Don't let the hurtful words of others make your day worse and take control of your mind. Think positively, cheer yourself up, surround yourself with optimistic and supportive people.

3. Use your words instead of your feelings

If someone is trying to wound your feelings, for example with passive-aggressive feedback, turn their words around and engage with the offender in constructive dialogue.

Don't forget you are allowed to interrupt and say: "Okay. I get it. There's a problem here. You have explained it very clearly. Can we talk about how to fix it? That's more helpful for both of us."

Overall, you are better off being a person who cares too much than a person who doesn't care at all. With luck, these sorts of workarounds can help provide cushions so that criticism doesn't hurt you too much.

Breaking stereotypes: educate men at work

I can imagine what it means for you to join a new dev team and be the only woman there—because I did it, three times. We're always being "welcomed" with the stereotypes. There is a general impression that men are better at "tech things," that they're more systematic and nuanced, and that on the other hand, women are more intuitive and better communicators, but their judgment isn't as solid.

A friend of mine works at the same digital media agency I used to work at. We often share our experiences and observations from working with each other. Once she told me, "You know, today when I was in a meeting about the project I'm working on, I sat at the table and said something. My team, all men, ignored my comment. Then I noticed whenever the male backend engineer spoke, everyone just stopped and listened. And I thought, that's what I want. I want people to take me seriously and respect my work."

Here's what she did next: she changed her job and started working for a company that values diversity. Now half of her engineering team is women. There she continues to work hard, learn new things and grow professionally. Based on my own experience, if you're new in the industry, the expectations placed on you can be burdensome. But if you're willing to work hard and understand that your first job probably won't be your dream job then it gets easier.

I firmly believe in diversity at work, not only of gender but also of experience level. For example, I believe in creating junior developer positions and training those juniors up. When they are fully integrated into the company, junior developers become loyal employees. By comparison, companies that only hire the most senior developers find that they often already have their own vision of how things have to work, which can be unproductive.

My friend's way worked for her, but she could have done it differently—break stereotypes, that is—by working to bring diversity to her former workplace. The following principles can help you do that.

Become an expert in a specific technology/approach and start advocating it

Currently my official title in the workplace is "Frontend Software Engineer." In my opinion, you can't be an expert front end developer just by knowing one thing. An expert developer is not necessarily skilled in any specific set of technologies; instead, they demonstrate the ability to learn new languages, frameworks and libraries as the need arises. The more they learn, the more they can compare and make informed decisions about what tech to pick and when.

Know the requirements of each situation. Don't be afraid of meeting a new challenge, even if you haven't solved that problem before. The more "unknown" things you learn and apply, the more your expertise will grow.

If you are fascinated by a technology, you can start to advocate it. Convince others to try it and use it. It will help you grow your credibility and break false stereotypes about women.

Increase your network of women and bring women engineers to the company

If you feel bad working on a team that's all men, what's stopping you from bringing a new woman colleague to your team?

Finding a woman developer is easier than it seems. You can start going to local meetups, volunteering at coding schools, joining university groups, and visiting other local tech events.

Companies are always passively looking for new people. It's normal for some people to leave the company and others to join, and someone will grow to the next level professionally and free up a junior position.

Help onboard new employees

This is the best way to learn and understand a project more deeply. Keep in mind that if you're a software developer at a product company, it's important to write clean and readable code so that even an intern can understand it—and by the way, you too, in case you return to that code in a week, a month or a year.

I want to talk about the mentor/mentee relationship, which isn't always strictly business. You can develop some real friendships when you take the time to advise someone and help them succeed.

When you develop a relationship with someone over time—when you help them, coach them, and guide them—that person's success is tied to you. Time after time, success will come back to you as the mentor.

Also, your protege can teach you from their own unique experiences and perspective, which may be very different from yours. They may also have new skills they can teach you.

People never forget their mentors.

Think back to when you first started working at your company. Wouldn't it have been nice to get some coaching from someone who had already been through that process?

Build trusting and professional relationships with colleagues and managers

In a company which incorporates people from diverse backgrounds into its network, each person has to trust the others to help them accomplish their own goals and the collective goal of the company.

That's why it's crucial to build trust within teams. It's a long process; it doesn't happen overnight.

The most likable and trustworthy people know that it's not worth offending people by expressing everything they know, even if they are correct. They're good listeners when someone else is talking.

It's also important to show empathy for your colleagues and keep an open mind. Do not judge— try to understand. Those who close themselves off from others' ideas are missing out not only on personal growth but also on opportunities for advancing their career.

People are different, and depending on the situation we may express ourselves differently, sometimes too emotionally. Try to learn how to maintain professional behavior in all circumstances. Overre- acting to things, either positively or negatively, will make a poor impression. Always remember that silence may be much more useful than angry words.

Women in code are driven. We want to prove ourselves. We want to work hard and grow, and it's impossible to buy that kind of enthusiasm.

In parting, I'd like to say: be the change you wish to see in our industry!

What to do when you're stuck

Isaac Lyman

Part of a programmer's job is chasing down missing semicolons and complex caching issues, scrutinizing and head-scratching over every line of code in an application. This is one of the most frustrating things about code: we use it to offload complexity from our brains, but the inverse of this benefit is that any useful program will be too complex for us to wrap our minds around completely. Complexity creates unknowns, and every unknown is a bug waiting to happen.

Another frustrating thing about code is that it has to be learned by rote. You're unlikely to discover the keyword or API you need by blind experimentation. And every language and library has gotchas, which may or may not be described in the documentation. There's no substitute for experience in situations like this.

Most programmers (I'd guess) are acquainted with the deep, hot, crushing frustration that ensues after hours of being stuck on a problem and not knowing how to progress. On that subject, here's a tweet from the guy who created Stack Overflow:

Source: https://twitter.com/codinghorror/status/695143348521140225[68]

This particular usage of my head has probably shortened my life expectancy by a few years. If you're a new programmer, you can avoid some of that by following a process similar to the one I'll recommend here. Each step builds on and escalates the one before it, and most of the time you'll get un-stuck long before you reach the last step.

1. Be self-aware

This will all go a lot better if you're taking care of yourself and paying attention to the way you feel. Sleep deprivation, hunger, a hostile work environment, or stressors in your personal life can directly affect your ability to solve problems. Ideally, you should be in a peaceful frame of mind when you start working. Then when you get frustrated, you can label the problem ("I'm stuck"), take a deep breath, and start on the path to resolving it.

---

[68]https://twitter.com/codinghorror/status/695143348521140225

To get off on the right foot, consider a morning routine that includes meditation and/or journaling. These can help you be more aware of your feelings.

2. Timebox your frustration

Once you've determined that you're stuck, set a timer for 20 minutes. Turn off Slack and email, put on your headphones, politely postpone questions and conversations with coworkers, and start Googling the problem. Read as much as you can about it. Try several different search queries. You may be surprised at how many other people have had your specific problem, even if it seems unique or proprietary. If you're lucky enough to have an error message, search it in quotes. Consider all the systems (libraries, packages, frameworks, APIs, services, etc.) that interact with the faulty part of the application, and ask yourself if the problem may be in a different place than you thought it was.

3. Rubber-duck it

Explain the problem to an imaginary coworker. Got a rubber duck or stuffed animal handy? Even better. I have a stuffed animal on my desk at all times. Describe the issue in as much detail as you can, and assume that your coworker isn't intimately familiar with the code you're talking about.

If this is hard for you, try composing an email or Slack message to a coworker that might be able to help. Don't send the message yet—just write it out and revise until you're satisfied that you've covered the problem in clear terms. Make sure to mention the research you've done and anything you've ruled out as the possible cause.

4. Draw it

On a piece of paper or a whiteboard, sketch out a basic diagram of the methods, classes and files that are interacting in the problem area. No fancy murals here—a bunch of circles and lines should be fine. Draw a piece of data traveling through this system as well. If you need to dig through the code a little to make sure your drawing is correct, take a minute to do so.

5. Take five

By now you should understand the problem pretty well (or know what you don't understand about it). At this point, put your computer to sleep and give your brain a rest. Anything that isn't mentally demanding will do. Strike up some light conversation with a friend or coworker, take a nap, go for a walk, get some lunch, watch a funny video, hit the gym, or take a shower. The solution may occur to you while you're doing something else entirely.

6. Ask for help

By now, you're reaching the limit of what you can do alone; you've probably spent 30-90 minutes on this problem. It's time to bring in reinforcements. Find a coworker who has relevant experience and ask for help. If you have no coworkers or none are available, reach out to your mentor. If you don't have a mentor, now's a good time to put that on your to-do list.

Don't worry about wasting their time. You've researched and thought through the problem, so you can describe it completely and succinctly. And for you to keep trying on your own could turn into a much more serious waste of time.

7. Isolate the problem

If you're still stuck, it's time to start from scratch. Create a small repository or use an online tool (like Codepen[69], Repl.it[70], or Stackblitz[71]) and see if you can add *just enough* code to reproduce the problem. One piece at a time, replicate the environment and code around the issue until you see it happen. Then try to remove various pieces, in turn, to make sure you haven't included anything unnecessary. What you'll end up with is the smallest possible example of the problem (an MCVE[72]), which will make it easier for someone to help you solve it. Review this with the person you asked for help in the previous step.

8. Write it up

Write a full description of the problem. Include code samples, a link to your repository or online code sample, screenshots (if applicable), and a summary of the things you've tried and the research you've done. Don't include anything that would pose a security risk to your company if it were posted publicly, because that's the next step.

9. Get a buddy and ask the internet

Find a buddy (possibly the person from step 6) and ask them to read through your writeup from step 8 to make sure it makes sense. Then post it on the internet. Stack Overflow and other Stack Exchange sites (like Server Fault, Software Engineering, or Database Administrators) are your best bet for getting a timely answer to your question, but their communities can be hostile to question askers, so don't go in alone—ask your buddy to upvote your question and help you defend against rude commenters or votes to close the question. With any luck, you'll get some good feedback and ideas within a day or two.

---

[69]https://codepen.io/
[70]https://repl.it/
[71]https://stackblitz.com/
[72]https://stackoverflow.com/help/mcve

10. Find a workaround

If you still haven't solved your problem, it's time for Plan B. You might consider altering the affected functionality, adding some fallback code, or switching to a different software library. This sounds a lot like giving up, but compromises are at the heart of all software, so don't beat yourself up over it.

Finally, document the solution

Once you've solved the problem, consider writing some documentation about it in order to alleviate someone else's frustration. This might be a comment in the code, a page on your company's internal docs, an email, a post on your blog or dev.to[73], or a self-answered Stack Overflow question.

And once again, keep an eye on your mental health. Programming is inherently frustrating. We all need breaks. If you're constantly getting burned out, it's time to take a day off, change your routine, or look for another job.

---

[73]https://dev.to/

Choosing a job title

Isaac Lyman

Are you a coder, programmer, developer, engineer, architect or something else?

My first job was an underage, under-the-table weekend gig at a pizza parlor. I'd show up at the local strip mall early Saturday morning, stash my bike, and clock in. For me, the work was grueling. I would haul 50-pound bags of flour and 10-gallon buckets of water to a giant stand mixer, and once it finished spinning I'd lift armfuls of incredibly heavy dough to a metal table where I'd cut and oil portions weighed for each size of pizza that the shop sold. By noon, I'd be exhausted. I'd clock out and head home. And once a month I'd pick up an envelope with about $100 cash in it. It was an awesome first job.

My official job title was Dough Boy (yes, like the Pillsbury mascot). But "Dough Boy" isn't very impressive on a resume, so for a while I listed my job title as "Dough Chef." A teenager's got to have some dignity, right? In the end, I don't think anybody cared.

Little did I know, that was the least problematic job title I would ever have.

I became a programmer several years ago. In 21st-century America—especially in the tech sector—job titles are surprisingly fluid. I haven't had an employer dedicate any real thought to my job title for a long time. In fact, my first employer in the industry told me I could put whatever I wanted on my resume and if anyone called she'd back me up. Naturally, I was tempted to write "Senior Department Lead QA III Technical Architect", when in fact I was just writing Selenium tests in a cubicle. Go figure.

I've often puzzled over the plethora of job titles I now fit under. I write web applications for a startup, so I do something at every level of the stack, from SQL Server at the bottom to CSS at the top. There are a lot of things I *could* call myself: coder, programmer, engineer, developer, boffin. In keeping with my pizza-infused legacy, I could even call myself a Software Boy[74]. So what *am* I?

---

[74]https://twitter.com/ivetwodads/status/854358415799312384

Source: https://twitter.com/jenlooper/status/854345325032747009[75]

I've discovered that I'm far from the only one who has this question. And there are a lot of variables to consider, so it's not an easy one. In some countries it's illegal to call yourself an engineer unless you have certain certifications. In some cultures, general words (like "consultant") may be preferred over technical jargon (like "application developer"). And in the United States, where I live, small differences in a job title can make a significant difference in salary.

This is my attempt to aggregate all the data I can find about the swath of job titles that apply to people who code. I've gathered average salary information and definitions for several job titles that might apply (but surely not all of them).

I've ignored titles like *hacker*, *ninja*, and *rockstar* because they're silly and meaningless.

Sources

I pulled salary information from the U.S. Bureau of Labor Statistics (BLS), Glassdoor, PayScale, and Indeed. Definitions come from the BLS or Wikipedia where available. Where neither has a definition, I've searched out the most succinct, authoritative source I can find.

Salary data

This data is categorized by job title. Job titles are ordered by a subjective estimate of their complexity, from least complex to most complex. Data was gathered in May 2019.

Each entry has a definition, national (USA) median salary data from each source, an average of the salary data points, and a variability assessment (how wide the range of salary estimates is). Where a specific job title or equivalent was not found in a database, "N/D" is used.

Statistical Note: PayScale.com uses the words "average" and "median" interchangeably. That's not how math[76] works, but oh well. Glassdoor and Indeed don't offer a median at all, preferring a much

[75]https://twitter.com/jenlooper/status/854345325032747009
[76]https://www.vocabulary.com/articles/chooseyourwords/mean-median-average/

less useful[77] average. In a perfect world everyone would use medians for data sets like this, since they may or may not follow a normal curve.

Coder

[A] person who writes computer code; a computer programmer. ~Dictionary.com[78]

Source	Salary
BLS	N/D
Glassdoor	$46,930[79]
Indeed	N/D
PayScale	N/D
Average	N/D
Variability	N/D

Notes: I'd usually avoid a site with so little street cred as Dictionary.com, but definitions for this word are surprisingly scarce.

Programmer

Create, modify, and test the code, forms, and script that allow computer applications to run. Work from specifications drawn up by software developers or other individuals. ~BLS[80]

Source	Salary
BLS	$84,280[81]
Glassdoor	$68,478[82]
Indeed	$73,643[83]
PayScale	$61,527[84]
Average	$71,982
Variability	Medium. Range of ~$22k.

Developer

[A] person or company that develops computer software. ~Merriam-Webster[85]

---

[77]https://surveymethods.com/blog/when-is-it-generally-better-to-use-median-over-mean/
[78]http://www.dictionary.com/browse/coder
[79]https://www.glassdoor.com/Salaries/coder-salary-SRCH_KO0,5.htm
[80]https://www.bls.gov/oes/current/oes151131.htm
[81]https://www.bls.gov/oes/current/oes151131.htm
[82]https://www.glassdoor.com/Salaries/programmer-salary-SRCH_KO0,10.htm
[83]https://www.indeed.com/salaries/Programmer-Salaries
[84]http://www.payscale.com/research/US/Job=Computer_Programmer/Salary
[85]https://www.merriam-webster.com/dictionary/developer

Source	Salary
BLS	N/D
Glassdoor	$80,394[86]
Indeed	$93,386[87]
PayScale	N/D
Average	$86,890
Variability	Medium. Range of ~$13k.

Notes: Several people have pointed out that the term "developer" could refer to someone in real estate as well as someone in software, so it's hard to know if these results are meaningful.

Front End Developer

A front-end developer is a type of computer programmer that codes and creates the visual front-end elements of a software, application or website. He or she creates computing components/features that are directly viewable and accessible by the end user or client. ~Techopedia[88]

Source	Salary
BLS	N/D
Glassdoor	$77,908[89]
Indeed	$102,297[90]
PayScale	$69,773[91]
Average	$83,326
Variability	Extreme. Range of ~$32k.

Web Developer

Design, create, and modify Web sites. Analyze user needs to implement Web site content, graphics, performance, and capacity. ~BLS[92]

Source	Salary
BLS	$69,430[93]
Glassdoor	$75,487[94]
Indeed	$72,644[95]
PayScale	$58,593[96]
Average	$69,038.50
Variability	Medium. Range of ~$15k.

[86]https://www.glassdoor.com/Salaries/developer-salary-SRCH_KO0,9.htm
[87]https://www.indeed.com/salaries/Developer-Salaries
[88]https://www.techopedia.com/definition/29569/front-end-developer
[89]https://www.glassdoor.com/Salaries/front-end-developer-salary-SRCH_KO0,19.htm
[90]https://www.indeed.com/salaries/Front-End-Developer-Salaries
[91]http://www.payscale.com/research/US/Job=Front_End_Developer_%2f_Engineer/Salary
[92]https://www.bls.gov/oes/current/oes151134.htm
[93]https://www.bls.gov/oes/current/oes151134.htm
[94]https://www.glassdoor.com/Salaries/web-developer-salary-SRCH_KO0,13.htm
[95]https://www.indeed.com/salaries/Web-Developer-Salaries
[96]http://www.payscale.com/research/US/Job=Web_Developer/Salary

Full Stack Developer

The term full-stack means developers who are comfortable working with both back-end and front-end technologies. To be more specific, it means that the developer can work with databases, PHP, HTML, CSS, JavaScript and everything in between, also, venturing as far as converting Photoshop designs to front-end code. ~George Fekete on SitePoint[97]

Source	Salary
BLS	N/D
Glassdoor	N/D
Indeed	$111,117[98]
PayScale	N/D
Average	N/D
Variability	N/D

Notes: There's[99] significant[100] doubt[101] as to whether this is a "real" job title, insofar as it refers to being an expert in several different layers of web technology. Given that Indeed is the only site to cough up a salary value, it seems that the industry shies away from it, whether for this reason or another one.

Software Developer

Develop, create, and modify general computer applications software or specialized utility programs. Analyze user needs and develop software solutions. ~BLS[102]

Source	Salary
BLS	$103,620[103]
Glassdoor	$80,018[104]
Indeed	N/D
PayScale	$69,928[105]
Average	$84,522
Variability	Extreme. Range of ~$33k.

Software Engineer

A software engineer is a person who applies the principles of software engineering to the design, development, maintenance, testing, and evaluation of the software and systems

---

[97]https://www.sitepoint.com/full-stack-developer/
[98]https://www.indeed.com/salaries/Full-Stack-Developer-Salaries
[99]https://dev.to/remotesynth/theres-no-such-thing-as-a-full-stack-developer-2fp9
[100]https://vitamintalent.com/blog/what-the-heck-is-a-full-stack-developer
[101]https://medium.com/@alexkatrompas/the-hard-truth-about-the-full-stack-developer-myths-and-lies-945ffadeeb8c
[102]https://www.bls.gov/oes/current/oes151132.htm
[103]https://www.bls.gov/oes/current/oes151132.htm
[104]https://www.glassdoor.com/Salaries/software-developer-salary-SRCH_KO0,18.htm
[105]http://www.payscale.com/research/US/Job=Software_Developer/Salary

that make computers or anything containing software work. ~Wikipedia[106]

Source	Salary
BLS	N/D
Glassdoor	$103,035[107]
Indeed	$107,366[108]
PayScale	$84,023[109]
Average	$98,141.33
Variability	Medium. Range of ~$23k.

Notes: In classic Wikipedia style, this definition is bafflingly circular. However, if you ignore the "principles of software engineering" part, the definition becomes useful.

This concludes a nearly-complete list of job titles that apply to regular devs. However, I'm going to go a bit further and see what "Junior", "Senior" and "Architect" do to a job title, even though these terms lie outside the mainstream.

Junior Software Developer

An entry-level engineer with limited exposure to development and development practice who will need strong mentoring and support to grow their skills. ~James Turnbull on Kartar.Net[110]

Source	Salary
BLS	N/D
Glassdoor	$64,962[111]
Indeed	$59,913[112]
PayScale	$59,579[113]
Average	$61,484.67
Variability	Very low. Range of ~$5k.

Senior Software Developer

...either someone with a deep specialised knowledge beyond their peers or someone who leads or instructs other developers. ~Robert Rees on The Guardian[114]

---

[106]https://en.wikipedia.org/wiki/Software_engineer
[107]https://www.glassdoor.com/Salaries/software-engineer-salary-SRCH_KO0,17.htm
[108]https://www.indeed.com/salaries/Software-Engineer-Salaries
[109]http://www.payscale.com/research/US/Job=Software_Engineer/Salary
[110]https://kartar.net/2015/09/so-what-exactly-is-a-junior-software-engineer/
[111]https://www.glassdoor.com/Salaries/junior-software-developer-salary-SRCH_KO0,25.htm
[112]https://www.indeed.com/salaries/Junior-Software-Developer-Salaries
[113]http://www.payscale.com/research/US/Job=Junior_Software_Engineer/Salary
[114]https://www.theguardian.com/info/developer-blog/2014/aug/28/what-does-it-mean-to-be-a-senior-developer

Source	Salary
BLS	N/D
Glassdoor	$95,791[115]
Indeed	N/D
PayScale	$101,732[116]
Average	$98,761.5
Variability	Very low. Range of ~$6k.

Software Architect

A software architect is a software expert who makes high-level design choices and dictates technical standards, including software coding standards, tools, and platforms. ~Wikipedia[117]

Source	Salary
BLS	N/D
Glassdoor	$132,510[118]
Indeed	$142,078[119]
PayScale	$121,645[120]
Average	$132,077.67
Variability	Medium. Range of ~$20k.

Analysis

Salaries

Job titles by salary from lowest to highest are:

- Junior Software Developer
- **Web Developer**
- **Programmer**
- Front End Developer
- **Software Developer**
- Developer
- Software Engineer
- Senior Software Developer
- Software Architect

[115]https://www.glassdoor.com/Salaries/senior-software-developer-salary-SRCH_KO0,25.htm
[116]http://www.payscale.com/research/US/Job=Sr._Software_Engineer_%2f_Developer_%2f_Programmer/Salary
[117]https://en.wikipedia.org/wiki/Software_architect
[118]https://www.glassdoor.com/Salaries/software-architect-salary-SRCH_KO0,18.htm
[119]https://www.indeed.com/salaries/Software-Architect-Salaries
[120]http://www.payscale.com/research/US/Job=Software_Architect/Salary

Coder and Full Stack Developer were lacking data. Since the BLS probably has the largest and least-biased data set, I've bolded the job titles that had BLS data available. Incidentally, the ordering of the list holds when BLS data is considered alone.

This data should be taken with a grain of salt for several reasons:

- I don't have access to the original data sets. I don't know the size of those data sets or the algorithms used to calculate their average/median. I don't have access to demographics data, so important variables like race, gender, orientation and class aren't considered here. A data set of known size and diversity would yield better analysis.
- Glassdoor and Indeed are fundamentally job boards, not public data sets. Their data is based on volunteered information: self-reported salaries and job postings. This makes it prone to several forms of survey bias.
- PayScale, Glassdoor and Indeed are private companies and their data isn't public. Any private company is accountable to its shareholders, not the general public, and may be incentivized to gather and calculate data in a way that increases the value of their product to customers. For example, employers posting jobs on Indeed may prefer the site to report lower average salary data, which would make their salary offers seem more competitive. Indeed could do this by focusing its marketing on regions with low cost of living and low average salary, which would skew its self-reported salary data toward the lower end of the scale. I'm not saying they do this, but it could be profitable for them to do so.

The difference in average salary between a Developer and a Software Developer is about $3k, which probably is not statistically significant. On the other hand, the difference between a Software Developer and a Software Engineer is $13k, which may be meaningful. The biggest leap in salary is from Senior Software Developer to Software Architect, with a difference of about $33k.

There are several more slight variations in wording that I could have looked into. A Senior Software Engineer, for example, probably makes a little bit more than a Senior Software Developer, and a Senior or Chief Software Architect surely makes more than a Software Architect. But this should be enough to provide insight into a general trend.

Definitions

Enough with the cash: what's the *qualitative* difference between these roles?

First of all, some titles to avoid (or at least approach with caution):

- *Coder* had the lowest Glassdoor salary of any position I looked at, even lower than Junior Software Developer. It's hard to argue in its favor. First of all, it's much too brazen—it's like a construction worker calling himself a Nailer or a doctor calling herself a Scalpeler. "Code" is better as a noun than a verb; it's a tool you use to achieve a goal. If a candidate for a position at my company billed themselves as a Coder, it would give me the impression that they like to be told what to do and how to do it—that is, they'll write the code, but they won't make decisions, interact with people, or suggest ways to improve. That sounds like an unfulfilling way to build software. What's worse, an employer who creates a job posting for a Coder probably isn't looking for someone who engineers elegant solutions to complex problems—they probably have only a shallow understanding of what software is, and want to hire the cheapest person they can find to "just build a really simple app."

- *Full Stack Developer* seems to beg the question, "but what are you *good* at?" As I've mentioned, people tend to be incredulous of a candidate who claims to be an expert at every level of the stack. There's simply no way a normal person can keep up with everything. And knowing a single technology at each layer (say, JavaScript, REST, .NET and SQL Server) probably doesn't cut it. Sure, those are the technologies in *your* stack, but someone else's stack may consist of Dart, Falcor, Python and Couchbase. You're not a Full Stack Developer where they're concerned. At best you're a regular Developer who's willing to learn some new tech.

- *(Computer) Programmer* is a term that's gone the way of the dinosaur, along with the stereotype of the shirt-and-tie-wearing geek in a cubicle. All the word really means[121] is *someone who knows a programming language*. This used to be a rare skill (and only moderately in demand). But modern software construction demands more than just syntax and vocabulary—the essential domains of "programming"—because modern *software* is more than just a command-line interface and a set of database files on a floppy disk. Apps have to be beautiful, accessible, user-friendly, fast, and above all, competitive. The word "Programmer" doesn't evoke any of that.

- *Developer* is, as previously noted, an unnecessarily ambiguous title. If your job involves building condominiums, you're reading the wrong book. If your job involves computer code, you should call yourself a *Software* Developer. Anything built with code is software, so this is more about clarification than qualification.

- *Front End Developer* is a very volatile title. Not only does it have almost the highest salary variability of all the job titles researched, but anecdotally I've heard it defined in contradictory ways. For some people, *Front End Developer* refers to a person who knows HTML and CSS but not JavaScript; for others, a Front End Developer is someone who has a deep knowledge of JavaScript and its most popular frameworks and libraries. The solution, in my mind, is to call yourself a *JavaScript Developer* if that's where your expertise lies, and to call yourself a *Web Designer* or *CSS Developer* if you specialize in HTML and CSS.

The remaining titles differ semantically, but not in ways that necessarily make any of them superior. You should determine which one best describes your career path:

- *Software Developer* and *Software Engineer* are, by many accounts, equivalent. Both mean that a person knows the best practices in their field, is comfortable with multiple technologies, and has transferable skills that allow them to recognize and write good code in any language. These titles also indicate the ability to make smart decisions about software design and implementation, and a willingness to participate in the software lifecycle above and beyond writing code (see "Development beyond the keyboard" for more on this topic). Developers and engineers are creative, thoughtful, knowledgeable people who deserve a place at the table in

---

[121]http://chrislema.com/programmer-developer-engineer/

every discussion about a product. "Engineer" connotes more seniority and preciseness than "Developer", so some would say that younger or less credentialed developers run the risk of sounding pretentious if they bill themselves as Engineers. But considering that the average salary difference between them is about $14k, I'd recommend using the term "Engineer" as long as there aren't any legal barriers to doing so.

- *Web Developer* is a title that flirts with ambiguity, if less dangerously than *Front End Developer*. I've seen the term used to mean "a person who builds web applications, including the server side" or just "a person who knows JavaScript." But as unclear as it is to industry insiders, it may be perfect for freelancers who cater to the "just make me a website" clientele. Most individuals and small business owners don't understand the complexities of front-end and back-end; if they hire a developer, it's to create an attractive single-purpose site that will show up in Google results. I suspect that *Web Developer* is exactly what they're looking for. If you're not a contractor, *Software Developer* may describe you more efficiently (and give you a $15k bump in average salary).

- *Junior* and *Senior* are prefixes that make a big difference in salary. Generally speaking, you're a *Junior Developer* for your first few years or so in the industry, and you're not a *Senior Developer* until a few years after that. But most developers agree that graduating from *Junior Developer* to *Developer* and from *Developer* to *Senior Developer* has less to do with the length of your career and more to do with your humility, leadership, versatility, and experience (especially the number of catastrophic failures under your belt).

- *Software Architect* is the most highly-paid job title on this list, and with good reason. It represents a high standard and has a stable definition industry-wide. The Software Architect is the ultimate technological resource—the person who's "been there and done that" so many times they can practically predict the future. At the last company where I worked, the Enterprise Architect was equal in status to the CTO. It's a position of extreme responsibility and respect. You probably already know if this is you.

- One more title I didn't investigate in depth is *x Developer* or *x Engineer*, where *x* is a specific language, framework or technology. For example, I could call myself a *JavaScript Developer*, a *Vue Developer*, or a *.NET Engineer*, and this would remove the ambiguity about what I'm primarily good at. I would choose one of the above based on my career goals, or combine two of them, e.g. *Vue / .NET Developer*. To look at every kind of *x Developer* would have increased the scope of this chapter far beyond its original purpose, but in my opinion it's the most useful job title there is for someone who codes. Of course, if you don't feel comfortable associating yourself with a specific technology, *Software Developer* is a totally acceptable alternative.

I hope the data I've provided helps you in the process of choosing your job title.

Bibliography & further reading

- The role of a Senior Developer, by Matt Briggs[122]. This is an excellent take on the skill metrics that various levels of developers should measure themselves against, rather than composing job titles based on years of experience.

---

[122]http://mattbriggs.net/blog/2015/06/01/the-role-of-a-senior-developer/

- When should you call yourself a senior developer? on Stack Exchange[123]. A few different takes on what makes a "senior" versus "junior" developer.
- What's the difference between Entry Level/Jr/Sr developers? on Stack Exchange[124]. Some worthy additions to the above.
- What does it mean to be a senior developer? on The Guardian[125]. What an above-average set of qualifications looks like.
- Programmer, Developer, Engineer: What's in a name? by Chris Lema[126]. A brief (and fairly representative) interpretation of the three main nouns in development job titles.
- Developer, Programmer or Engineer? on Stack Overflow Talent[127]. Some survey data and well-considered quotes from industry insiders.
- Job Titles in the Web Industry, by Chris Coyier on CSS-Tricks[128]. I think the distinctions here may be a little too rigid, but to ignore Coyier's take on the subject would be a significant omission. At the very least, this is a good reference on what various titles *should* mean.
- What Does a Software Architect Do? by Yegor Bugayenko[129]. This article proposes that being a software architect isn't just about smarts or experience, it's about accountability and responsibility.
- The Role of Software Architect, by Bredemeyer Consulting[130]. Frames the architect as part technologist, part business strategist—meaning that the sharpest dev in the company may or may not be a good fit for the job.

---

[123]https://softwareengineering.stackexchange.com/q/25564
[124]https://softwareengineering.stackexchange.com/questions/14914/whats-the-difference-between-entry-level-jr-sr-developers
[125]https://www.theguardian.com/info/developer-blog/2014/aug/28/what-does-it-mean-to-be-a-senior-developer
[126]http://chrislema.com/programmer-developer-engineer/
[127]https://www.stackoverflowbusiness.com/blog/developer-programmer-or-engineer
[128]https://css-tricks.com/job-titles-in-the-web-industry/
[129]http://www.yegor256.com/2014/10/12/who-is-software-architect.html
[130]http://www.bredemeyer.com/who.htm

The DevOps introduction I wish I had

Periklis Gkolias

Buzzwords are common in this industry. They're used everywhere (sometimes in the wrong way) and because of that, people are often afraid to ask 101-level questions as they don't want to sound ignorant.

Some years ago, my manager asked me if I wanted to do some DevOps work as part of my software engineer job. Of course, I was young and afraid to ask what that meant so I just said "yeah, let's give it a try. Worst case scenario, I will die and you can take a day off to grieve."

Thank God, I am still alive, as you have probably noticed. So now I want to give you a nice round overview of the terms I encountered in my initial foray into DevOps and wish I knew back then.

Till not many years ago...

As software engineers, we write software on our computers for other people. And that is problem number one. The software will eventually have to run on someone else's computer because the end user doesn't have access to our computer. And this is a good thing; imagine the security implications if anyone could access your computer.

But the end user doesn't care how well the software works on our computer. They care how it works on theirs. If we want to do something meaningful and maybe make some money, *we have to put our software out in public.*

But who will do this job? Till not many years ago, it was up to the "operations people" of the company. I might be oversimplifying here, but you can think of them as colleagues from the IT department that had a technical background but weren't coders or managers. For example, server administrators[131] and database experts[132].

Can you see a problem here? Think about that and I'll explain in a moment.

DevOps

The DevOps discipline was created to bridge the gap between developers and operations people, the groups discussed above. The goal is for the transition from a developer's computer to the public to be mostly quick, flawless, trackable, and repeatable, with as little as possible manual work. You may hear this transition referred to as the *deployment* of the application.

---

[131]https://en.wikipedia.org/wiki/Server_administrator
[132]https://en.wikipedia.org/wiki/Database_administrator

Before that, deployments caused constant disagreement and blame between the two tribes. They were slow and painful and required lots of working hours. This is the problem I mentioned in the previous section.

The operations people often had no clue why the app couldn't be deployed even though they were doing everything they were supposed to do; after all, they didn't write it or understand the internals. And the developers were blaming the operations people because "it works on my computer."

Starting in 2001 there was huge movement (called the Agile manifesto[133]) to improve the way we produce software and provide it to the public. The DevOps discipline was born as a side effect of that.

The public

What is this terrifying "public" that led all those poor operations people to exhaust themselves working overtime? At the time of writing, when people are speaking about deployments, they usually mean deploying an application to a cloud server so that anyone with a URL (more or less) can access it.

The cloud? What is the cloud?

When it comes to software engineering, it basically means "another company's computer." Giant companies like Microsoft (with Azure[134]), Amazon (with AWS[135]) and Google (with Google Cloud[136]) have thousands of servers running to support their business, as do some smaller companies.

Some of those computers are rented out for others to use and the users (usually companies that don't have such high-quality infrastructure and don't want to buy it) are charged accordingly, *based on how much time they occupy it for*. This offers a few advantages and disadvantages, but those are outside the scope of this chapter.

What is the main problem when deploying to the cloud?

A major problem, as mentioned before, was that there was no guarantee that if a feature was running on the computer of the original developer then it would run equally well on the cloud.

This can happen because of missing libraries, different library versions between the two machines, or even because the local computer runs on a different operating system than the server, to name a few examples.

Running an application in various operating systems

This is actually very common. Let's say you're at a company where the CTO used to work for Microsoft, so having Windows workstations is something they are not willing to negotiate.

---

[133]https://agilemanifesto.org/principles.html
[134]https://azure.microsoft.com
[135]https://aws.amazon.com/
[136]https://cloud.google.com/

Let's also say one of your major customers is a giant Linux software company. As you can imagine, they're guaranteed to have Linux servers on their infrastructure.

What do you do? Do you switch to Linux or make them switch to Windows? *Neither scenario is viable.* What if you had hundreds of customers which all had different operating systems in their infrastructure? How do you make your applications run well for all of them?

There are various approaches to solve this problem. It's one of the main concerns of not only a DevOps engineer but also the whole team.

Docker and containers in general

The most popular solution goes by the name "containerization." Containerization is an approach where you enclose everything you need (literally everything) in a software "box" (or container) in order for the software to run smoothly.

The container, for the sake of simplicity, can be thought of like a tiny operating system that runs on top of your existing one and is completely portable.

You can move a container from computer to computer (and of course to a cloud server). If it works on one computer, it will also work on another, equally well, with no strings attached. The only prerequisite is to have the appropriate container technology like Docker[137] installed.

So for example, in order to solve the aforementioned issue, we could follow this approach (which is very common):

- Create a container using your preferred operating system.
- Include the source code of our app in the container.
- Include the libraries our application needs, along with any other piece of software our app relies on.
- Configure the container so that when it is accessed, the app starts automatically.
- Test the application thoroughly from inside the container.
- Once happy, send it to the customer(s). You are now confident that it will work on their side too, regardless of the operating system they use.

Note: When it comes to Docker, we distinguish between a container and the file that runs inside of it with the terms "Docker container" and "Docker image."

Another famous solution is Packer[138] by Hashicorp[139]. Feel free to read about them and see what works best for you when the time comes.

---

[137]https://www.docker.com/
[138]https://www.packer.io/
[139]https://www.hashicorp.com/

Docker vs. virtual machines

A virtual machine or VM is a standalone operating system that is treated as a normal application by the host operating system. You can interact with it as if it were your actual environment and forget about the host.

Yes, Docker[140] and VMs solve similar problems. They don't work in the same way though, and Docker is often the preferred approach nowadays.

The most important differences lie in their size and the way they utilize the host operating system. For example, Docker is usually much more lightweight and tends to share more functionality with the host operating system than a VM.

Provisioning

"Provisioning" is another term you might encounter and be too afraid to ask what it is.

In the DevOps context, it means to set up the infrastructure needed for an application to work. This work is often automated and done in the cloud.

So if someone wants to provision a test environment, they probably have to allocate some server space in order to put the containers inside and run them. If done manually, this can be a tedious process.

Thankfully, there are provisioning tools on the market that do the job for you fairly easily, or at least with minimal input (apart from the initial configuration).

Continuous Integration and Continuous Delivery (CI/CD)

Those two terms refer to an organization's need to know if newly-written code has problems and if not, to be able to send it to the customer in an automated way, whenever they want. It's a common practice and you should have a high-level understanding of it.

Here is how this works:

- You create a new feature requested by a customer.
- Your code gets reviewed and tested by members of your team.
- You add your changes to the code that will be delivered to the customer (the "release branch," as devs call it).
- An automated process notices what you did and starts doing various things with the new version of the app, like trying to compile it, run any automated tests, and (you guessed it) prepare your Docker image. This is the "Continuous Integration" step.
- If everything works, the process sends this image to the customer's servers. This is the "Continuous Delivery" step.

---

[140]https://www.docker.com/

Some of the most well-known CI/CD tools are Jenkins[141], Travis[142], and Bamboo[143].

Tips for the future

Before closing this chapter, I would like to give you a couple of tips that you might find helpful during your first years in tech.

- If you don't understand something, Google it. If you can't figure it out easily, ask. No one expects you to know everything and you never have to. If someone has told you otherwise, you're in the wrong company.
- Automate as much as you can. Anything that has to be done manually is error-prone and far more time consuming.
- Never stop learning. DevOps is a great field and is evolving rapidly. You need to keep your knowledge up to avoid becoming outdated or obsolete.

---

[141]https://jenkins.io/
[142]https://travis-ci.org/
[143]https://www.atlassian.com/software/bamboo

A coder's code of ethics

Isaac Lyman

Code can do amazing things. We're all the beneficiaries of it: computers, cell phones, the internet, MRI machines—it's hard to imagine a world without software.

Code can also do bad things. It can lie, steal, murder, surveil and discriminate. In fact it's done all of these things, wielded by programmers like you and me, programmers who sometimes didn't understand what they were being asked to do and other times didn't care. Unless you're very lucky, at some point in your career you'll be asked to develop a feature that seems questionable or even just plain wrong. What will you do?

Will you rationalize it to yourself? It's not like the feature was your idea. Your bosses sign the paychecks, so they call the shots. It would be them in trouble, not you. Right?

Or will you take a stand? You're not some mindless soldier.

The decision is up to you, but you may find that "I was just following orders" isn't a very good defense in a courtroom, much less against your own conscience.

Several writers have considered the need for a code of ethics in programming. In my research for this chapter I studied the Hippocratic Oath, perhaps the most famous ethical code in any profession. Its ideals include knowledge-sharing, humility, and good citizenship. (If you're interested, check it out on Wikipedia[144].) These are great things to start with, but there is much more to discuss. Following are some of the things to watch out for as you strive to be an ethical programmer.

Privacy

Privacy advocates have been railing against Facebook since the beginning[145]. Even the News Feed, which we now take for granted, was once seen as invasive—and one reason we take it for granted is because much bigger problems are rocking the social media platform on a regular basis, like the still-fresh Cambridge Analytica scandal[146]. And Facebook isn't the only company in the doghouse: Google[147], Amazon[148], Uber[149] and many others have spent time in the news for failing to protect user data.

How did they go so wrong? There are a few factors at work here.

---

[144]https://en.wikipedia.org/wiki/Hippocratic_Oath#Modern_versions_and_relevance
[145]https://www.nbcnews.com/tech/social-media/timeline-facebook-s-privacy-issues-its-responses-n859651
[146]https://en.wikipedia.org/wiki/Facebook%E2%80%93Cambridge_Analytica_data_scandal
[147]https://en.wikipedia.org/wiki/Privacy_concerns_regarding_Google
[148]https://www.washingtonpost.com/technology/2018/12/20/amazon-alexa-user-receives-audio-recordings-stranger-through-human-error/?noredirect=on
[149]https://www.theverge.com/2017/8/15/16150902/uber-ftc-complaint-mishandle-privacy-data

First, collecting user data is incredibly easy—you can collect a user's name, phone number, home address, government ID number or anything else they're willing to give you in only a few lines of code. Storing and retrieving data is so essential to computer applications that enormous sums of money have been spent engineering APIs and platforms to make it easier. It's almost the default thing to do in most cases, only a couple steps behind displaying words on a screen.

Second, protecting user data is much harder, requiring both expertise and intent. In order to prevent a password from being stolen, you have to know at least a few things about databases, cryptography, one-way hashes, and secure transmission. And then you have to apply them consistently across an entire system, no matter how large or complex it becomes. An application's security is only as strong as its weakest point, so this requires continuous investment. And security is generally inconvenient; if a customer calls in because they forgot their password, it may seem easier to just tell it to them rather than making them follow a password reset process over email. But no secure system will ever allow you to *see* their password, let alone tell it to them.

Third, for businesses, "hard" and "expensive" are synonyms. And if no one in leadership is willing to make a principled stand, a corporation will always choose money over human rights. This is exacerbated by the fact that user data is worth a lot on the open market. Advertisers will do almost anything to obtain people's private information, and much of the software we use (especially free software) is wholly dependent on advertising.

These factors in combination make a perfect storm: it's cheap, easy, convenient, and profitable to collect oodles of user data and store it practically in the open. And the consequences, although certain, are never immediate. It's easy to forget that there are consequences at all.

Ethics demands more of us. As programmers, we should refuse to collect more data than our applications need. We should take users' trust seriously and protect what they give us. We should be sensitive to the kinds of data that are especially private and be especially diligent in protecting them. We should educate ourselves in security best practices. When hackers come looking for easy pickings (and they will) we should be confident that they'll leave empty-handed.

Preventing bugs and outages

Most software is "line of business" software: applications people use on a daily basis to do their jobs. When you write this kind of application, you're holding a workforce's productivity in your hands. A bug, outage, or unnecessarily slow algorithm can cost someone several working days. That's a lot of responsibility.

Additionally, you probably know the frustration of buying an app or video game only to find that it doesn't work very well—maybe there are tons of bugs, or the servers go down a lot, or it loses all your data for no reason. You feel cheated, and rightly so. The developer made you an unspoken promise when they sold you the software, and now you're left to deal with their carelessness.

Some software does damage when it works. Most software does damage when it's broken. There are many things we can do to avoid shipping broken software, but in general we should test every release ahead of time with the assumption that it's broken in some way. Then we should fix it before releasing. Automated tests, quality assurance, redundancy, monitoring, and automated rollbacks can help reduce the frequency and impact of severe bugs (see Appendix A for definitions of these terms).

There's a huge difference between teams that take this seriously and teams that don't. And it isn't always the developers' fault; if your boss is setting impossibly tight deadlines, making you work overtime, or demanding you ship new features as quickly as possible, everything is going to be broken every day. You simply won't have the time or energy to keep your software bug-free. A company that runs like this is in serious trouble. But in most situations, you can make a difference by advocating for quality assurance and testing best practices. And this helps you keep your promises to your users.

Avoiding dark patterns

A "dark pattern" is any feature of a user interface (UI) intended to trick users into doing (or not doing) something. Many dark patterns rely on users not paying close attention to every detail and every block of text in an application—and seriously, who does? If you've ever opted into something you didn't want because there was a "big green button," or accidentally clicked an ad when you were trying to make it go away, you're the victim of a dark pattern.

The first rule of UI design is "users don't read" (or, alternately, "users don't think"[150]). This can be an inconvenience—we can't just use paragraphs of text to tell users exactly what to do. We have to make it *obvious* what the user should do through the careful use of color, contrast, sizing, positioning, and iconography (and yes, text, but usually only a word or two at a time). This is hard, which is one reason why designers are so valuable. But generally a dark pattern isn't the result of a simple oversight or design mistake. It's an intentional attempt to take advantage of users' trust in order to hijack their time, attention, or wallet. And it's incredibly common.

File sharing and download sites are full of dark patterns. Sometimes there are so many "Download" buttons it's nearly impossible to figure out which ones are ads in disguise and which one is real. And many news and media sites are almost as bad, with so many ads and newsletter signup forms you can't see the content you came for. But even the most well-known sites on the web—Facebook, LinkedIn, and TurboTax, for example—are notorious for their use of dark patterns to get users to give up personal information, share contact lists, or pay for a service advertised as free.

Another kind of dark pattern relies not on tricking the user into doing something they don't mean to, but on making it difficult to do something they *do* mean to. Several major brands—like Blue Apron, Marriott Hotels, and the New York Times—have recently been called out for making it incredibly hard to unsubscribe from their emails or services, often requiring a lengthy phone call and identity verification even though they allow you to sign up online with only a few clicks. If that isn't bad enough, most advertisers and data brokers will collect information about your internet browsing habits without your permission or knowledge, effectively "signing you up" for a service you didn't even know existed—and you usually can't close your account with them, regardless of how much you may want to.

---

[150]http://sensible.com/dmmt.html

We may not be designing the apps we write, but we should still insist on ethical design standards. There's no excuse for employing underhanded tactics to trick our users or trap them into an arrangement they want to leave.

Impartiality and accessibility

We're tempted to think of computers as completely unbiased and objective, but this assumption is problematic: it leads to systems that perpetuate our own biases and those of the world around us. Computers may not be born with an understanding of racism, sexism, ableism, or classism, but unfortunately, you can't avoid bias just by being ignorant of it.

Our default approach to algorithms that deal with people may be to treat each of them as a data point, completely equal in the eyes of the code. But this lofty ideal falls apart as soon as we introduce a user interface, business logic, or artificial intelligence. Technical equality is not the same as fairness.

A blind user and a sighted user might be treated as equal data points by our code, but if we don't build accessibility into our UI, the blind user will be unable to use the software. Our equality is their disadvantage. This isn't the computer's bias, it's ours, manifested in code.

An application's database might not store information about sexual identity, race, or social class, but due to differences and biases in the real world, the software can effectively discriminate on any of these bases by making assumptions about the user's physical size, sexual preference, skin contrast, living arrangements, or access to a cell phone.

Artificial intelligence is especially prone to bias. Amazon learned this the hard way[151] in 2018, when it tried teaching an AI to select job candidates similar to the people they had already hired. The AI quickly learned that most of their employees were men, so it started discounting resumes with the word "women" or the names of certain women's colleges on them. This was an egregious case of sexual discrimination. But AI can be even more insidious, using much less obvious data points as proxies for race and sex. Something as innocuous as a zip code can enable discrimination unless careful controls are in place.

It's our job to watch for and avoid these issues. And we're likely to fail unless we have people on our development teams who don't look like us—people of other races, sexes, levels of ability, and socioeconomic backgrounds. A combination of awareness, diversity, and broad user testing is the best way to ensure our applications are truly impartial and accessible to all kinds of users.

Do no harm

The famous phrase *primum non nocere* ("first do no harm") is a core tenet of the medical profession. It should also be a tenet of ours. It's important to consider the human cost of every development project. Some software, whether by design or by lack of foresight, does harm in real and immediate ways.

---

[151]https://www.aclu.org/blog/womens-rights/womens-rights-workplace/why-amazons-automated-hiring-tool-discriminated-against

Weapons are a case in point. No modern missile takes flight without a team of engineers behind it. That's a heavy responsibility, to write code knowing that it will end lives. No one would blame you for refusing to be part of such a project. The ethics of military force are a topic of debate, but wherever human casualties are involved, we'd better be prepared to account for our decisions.

Malware is a more clear-cut example: few of us would attempt an ethical argument to justify the creation of viruses and ransomware. Yet malware is a fixture in the modern world, a constant threat to our digital well-being. WannaCry[152], a piece of ransomware that made headlines in 2017, infected thousands of computers throughout Great Britain's National Health Service and forced hospitals to turn some patients away. It also halted production at certain factories and automotive plants. Thanks to some high-quality security research and a few lucky breaks, the impact of WannaCry was relatively low. But it's easy to imagine a much worse scenario: unusable MRI machines, hundreds dead from health complications, frozen supply chains, mass layoffs, abrupt economic collapse in some sectors, and so on. The creators of WannaCry appeared to be spreading it for their own financial gain, requesting a few hundred dollars per victim. But there are credible allegations that they were agents of the North Korean government, which makes the attack a potential act of war.

Make no mistake, you don't need to be programming a ballistic missile to be dealing with life and death.

Of a less catastrophic nature (but still decidedly bad) is software that uses your computer's resources in ways you wouldn't appreciate, like 2018's spate of cryptojacking[153]—a word describing applications that secretly use your processor to mine Bitcoin, enriching their creator while leaving you with an inflated electricity bill, wear and tear on your hardware, and a slower computer. This is more petty theft than high crime, but that doesn't make it victimless.

Perhaps the trickiest time to apply "do no harm" is when we're making tools that rely on user-generated content. Twitter and Facebook, for example, are irreplaceable parts of many peoples' personal and professional lives. The amount of good-natured media and humor generated daily on the sites is impressive. But they're also used daily to harass women, LGBT people, and people of color. They're used to encourage acts of group violence and suicide. They're depressing and addictive[154] to users. There are tools that allow users to report the worst cases of abuse, but moderation is spotty at best—and the people who do it suffer severe mental and emotional consequences[155]. In these circumstances, we'd be justified in asking if social media should exist at all.

Even in the simplest of situations "do no harm" is an essential standard. Any software that helps a doctor do their job, even something as innocuous as a file-sharing server or document editor, can become urgently important in a patient's life during a medical crisis. A bug or bad UX could lead to injury or death. The same goes for air traffic controllers, taxi drivers, manufacturers—even small-time retailers stand to lose a great deal if their software is broken. Regardless of what you're building, the user's worst case scenario may only be a few lines of code away.

---

[152]https://en.wikipedia.org/wiki/WannaCry_ransomware_attack
[153]https://www.nbcnews.com/tech/tech-news/your-computer-could-be-quietly-mining-bitcoin-someone-else-n922101
[154]https://www.marketwatch.com/story/new-study-claims-facebook-instagram-and-snapchat-are-linked-to-depression-2018-11-09
[155]https://www.cnet.com/news/facebook-content-moderation-is-an-ugly-business-heres-who-does-it/

These are concerns you should take with you to each job interview and each project. We should insist on writing applications that are reliable, make the world better, earn users' trust, and are thoughtful about the ways they allow people to interact.

The golden user story

I often hear stories of CEOs who refuse to let their kids use software produced by *their own companies*. And this illustrates perhaps the most essential principle of all: if you wouldn't want an app to do something to your child or significant other or friend, then don't make that app.

We have the ability to make software that enriches lives and creates opportunities. And as Marc Andreessen famously said, software is eating the world. We, the next generation of programmers, can decide what the future looks like. It all depends on the code we write today.

Software development beyond the keyboard

Isaac Lyman

One of the greatest paradoxes of software development is the relative unimportance of code. As engineers we study code, we teach about code, we agonize over code, we go to conferences and debate each other and dream vivid dreams about code. Yet there is no line of code in any programming language that will make a company profitable or an idea successful. Applications are of course valuable, and largely responsible for the experiences that shape the modern world, but most applications could be equally useful if they were written in a different programming language, under a different paradigm, using different techniques and algorithms. There are infinite ways to write a program. Sometimes one way is faster than another, sometimes more readable, sometimes more error-resistant. But usually it's just different.

In many people's minds, then, the difference between a good developer and a great developer isn't about how quickly or correctly they write code. It's about skills beyond the keyboard: communication, leadership, reasoning. Following are a few skills you can learn to raise your value in the workplace.

Asking hard questions

Code hates ambiguity, which is one of the main reasons coding is hard. If you want to code an *idea*, you have to convert it to an *algorithm*, which requires imagining it on a deep level: what are the steps from beginning to end? How will you accommodate different users, different privileges, different devices? How will the application know what it needs to know? What if something goes wrong? What if the user does something unexpected? What if a hacker is trying to get in?

CEOs and managers usually think about products and features on a high level (and they should). They'll say something like "we need a button that lets people export their data as an Excel spreadsheet." They see this feature as if it were under a spotlight in a dark room; it seems so simple. Your job as a programmer is to listen to them, stand in the spotlight with them and understand their vision, and then grab a flashlight and explore the dark, dusty corners of the room. What should the spreadsheet be called? What columns should it have? Does it need access controls? Should the application warn the user if their data is empty, or corrupt, or larger than 100 megabytes? Is Excel even the best way to handle this kind of data? Would a CSV file be acceptable instead, since it's easier to generate?

Sometimes the questions need to dig even deeper. Is this feature worth two months of our team's time and effort? What problem are we actually trying to solve (see Appendix A, "XY Problem")?

Are we sure this will solve it? Are customers asking for this? What problem are *they* trying to solve? And so on. Some questions you can answer on your own, but many will need to be discussed by management. Sometimes you'll have to explain your question several times before anyone understands it. Sometimes they never will, and you'll need to ask a different one.

This may not be coding, but it's software development in the truest sense. It's part of the painful but necessary process of making software *real*, and it's something that can only be done by people like us: people who are methodical and thoughtful, people who see the smallest details and sense problems before they happen. It's a talent that runs strong among coders, and one you can develop if you haven't yet.

As a new programmer, you may feel nervous about asking questions that risk putting your lack of experience on display. It's normal to feel that way, but don't let it silence you. If you prefer, you can take the questions you're most insecure about to your dev lead, mentor, or manager, one-on-one. But keep in mind that your inexperience is in many ways an asset—you have a fresh perspective and haven't developed the same blind spots that many of your senior colleagues may have. And even the most senior of programmers asks a dumb question now and then.

Contributing to UX and feature discussions

Some managers see developers as nothing more than code-producing machines, relegating them to the last step in a lengthy design process. This often backfires. Without a developer in the room, it's difficult to know what is easy and what is impossible, what adds complexity and what reduces it, what it costs to build something *good enough* versus *perfect*.

Developers are master problem-solvers. Coding is, after all, an exercise in working with constraints, tradeoffs, and outcomes. The best companies recognize this skill and ask for developers' input throughout the entire product development process, from design to delivery.

If you can, take the opportunity to sit in on high-level product discussions. If you pitch in now and then with "that's an expensive feature—could we do it like this instead?" or "that's a great idea, but it will take some effort. Could we validate it with a few users first?" or "that's simple, I can build it in an afternoon," you'll quickly find yourself indispensable in the process. This is perhaps the place where your skills make the biggest difference: not hunched over a keyboard, staring at an IDE until your eyes blur, but at the table with product managers and executives, representing the possibilities and limitations of code as everyone plans ways to improve customers' lives.

Talking to users

A famous moment in the tech world occurred in 2001, when a group of 17 software professionals gathered in Utah, USA, and agreed on a set of core principles to guide the development of software in the Internet Age.

...we have come to value:

Individuals and interactions over processes and tools

Working software over comprehensive documentation

Customer collaboration over contract negotiation

Responding to change over following a plan

~ *Manifesto for Agile Software Development*

The last two values, "customer collaboration" and "responding to change," point to one of the most important processes a software company can adopt: regularly speaking to customers about their needs, then updating priorities and plans to accommodate them better. Companies that fail to do this may produce high-quality software but most of the time it won't be very useful. Developers spend a lot of time worried about "building things wrong"—writing bugs or misunderstanding specifications, for example—but an even bigger problem is "building the wrong things." If your app doesn't solve my problem, I don't care if it's the most beautiful and bug-free app in the universe.

As a developer, you could argue that it's not your job to speak to users and gather feedback. The problem is that in too many organizations, *nobody* thinks it's their job (although good UX designers or product owners will usually take it on). In reality it should be everyone's job: every part of the process exists to provide a better experience for users, so everyone has a stake in understanding them. For a deeper discussion of this topic, see Edaqa's chapter "You are an interpreter".

Writing documentation

Poor, out-of-date or nonexistent documentation is the status quo for much of the tech industry. This causes endless headaches for managers. When a developer leaves after a long employment, they take knowledge with them that no one else has. When a new developer joins the team, it takes them months to get up to speed. When two teams work together, they end up spending tens of hours sharing knowledge face to face. Even in a small company with low turnover, "mental turnover" is still expensive—I don't remember the details of what I was working on a year ago, do you? It might as well have been another life.

If you know how to write clear and organized documentation, you can reduce these expenses dramatically. Documenting the setup process for new developers can help a recently-hired teammate contribute much sooner. Documenting the architecture of a system and its core assumptions and constraints can create an invaluable roadmap for developers tackling complex issues. Creating an FAQ for bugs or error messages that frequently appear can save your teammates days of unnecessary debugging. Whenever you or one of your teammates asks "how does that work again?" that's a sure sign documentation is needed.

Writing is hard, so don't be afraid to take the easy route: use lots of bullet points, throw in a drawing or diagram here and there, overexplain things a little, and ask your team to review and edit what you've written.

One of the most powerful and respectful ways to leave your job is with a digital stockpile of excellent documentation behind you. Once you give notice, insist on taking the time to write things down:

everything you built alone, everything you were the expert on, everything people asked you to explain on a regular basis. Your coworkers will be thanking you until long after you're gone.

Code design

Speaking of documentation, one of the best ways to develop both faster and smarter is to plan out your solutions ahead of time. At a previous job, we called this a "dev design." The developer assigned to a task would write a summary of the code they planned to write, including a breakdown of sub-tasks, a list of every file they planned to change, method signatures, class and field names, table schemas, and—for especially tricky situations—even a few lines of pseudocode (see Appendix A for definitions of these terms). Then they would take 20 minutes to review it with the team. This was the most productive meeting of our day. More often than not, we'd save each other *hours* of development time by saying things like "we already have a class that does that, we can reuse it" or "that's a tricky procedure, watch out for race conditions" or "I don't think that's what was intended with that feature, let's talk to our manager and clarify it."

At that company, we further justified the time spent on dev designs by doing away with formal code reviews. If our dev design turned out to be inadequate once we started coding, we would update it and notify the team. This way, the actual code being written was never a surprise—it was "pre-approved." Replacing code reviews may not make sense for most teams, but when building new products and features, I tend to believe that code design ahead of time is more valuable than code review after the fact. Of course, it doesn't have to be an either/or situation. On my current team we do both.

Even if your team isn't friendly to the idea, doing code design on your own has compelling benefits. It helps you avoid rewrites by making sure all the parts of your solution work together conceptually. It helps you find blockers sooner, so you can stay productive while they're being resolved. It gives you a record of why you coded things the way you did, so in six months when you're refactoring or extending a feature, you can remember the constraints you were working with.

Development isn't just code

To call yourself a software developer is to claim the whole development process as your own. Don't forget that code is only one step of many in that process, and it's near the end. Becoming proficient in the other steps will make you a more well-rounded and valuable asset at every job you take.

Code reviews

Rosalind Thuy Pham

What is a code review?

Code Review is an activity performed by developers after finishing a feature or bug fix. A developer requests a review from their peers. Depending on the impact of the code to the current code base, it may require more than one developer to review.

Why do we do code reviews?

In software development, an application is broken down by features. A feature can be isolated or depend on another feature. To ensure each feature is added without defects or side effects, developers request a code review from their peers or voluntarily review each other's code.

In most cases, reviewing code means validating and checking for code quality violations. However, in many collaborative companies, code review is also seen as a way to share domain knowledge within a team. Through code review, senior developers can share high-level understanding with junior developers to avoid duplicate code and improve performance. Junior developers can also review others' code. It's an excellent chance to see how others have applied code guidelines and to learn best practices.

Who should review a junior developer's code?

Any developer on their team. If the code is implementing a new feature, the junior developer should pick a senior developer who recently worked on a related area of the code. Early involvement of a senior developer can make the code review go more smoothly. If the code is a bug fix or improvement, like a typo, missing variable, or wrong type, the reviewer can be any available team member.

How should you review someone's code?

Ideally, the developer who wrote the code and their peers should have discussed the feature or bug fix and designed the overall solution before the code was written. Understanding the context and conceptualizing the solution are far more important than making the code pretty. Good planning helps to avoid wasted time and effort if the requirements change or a solution already exists.

There are many possible solutions to most problems. At this point, reviewers and code authors should feel that they both understand and agree on the chosen solution. Next, they should both agree on the logic of that solution.

When viewing the code for the first time, reviewers refer back to the written product requirements to get some context around the code and use a diff tool to identify the logic of the solution. For example, say the solution is an input field for a user to type their name. The logic could be a function which captures each key press and its value. This is a simple example, but the logic of a solution can span multiple functions in different files. Reviewers should ask questions or leave comments based on their impression of the code.

For many junior developers, this might be their first time receiving feedback on their work. Therefore, some questions and comments may sound more sarcastic and offensive than they are. Here are some example questions:

- "Why do you need these?"
- "I don't think it makes sense to add this line."
- "I don't understand what this function is trying to do."

Discussing someone else's work is not easy, and not all developers are excellent communicators. My best advice for junior developers is to focus on what you've learned at the end of the day, not what people might think about you. The fact is the more feedback you receive, the more you learn, and the better you figure things out. It's hard to take criticism, but it's better than no feedback at all.

The developer who submitted the pull request (the author) should read and respond to each question and comment. If necessary, the author and reviewers can have a discussion in person, over the phone, or while pair programming to explain the solution to reviewers.

At the end of this step, the author and reviewers should agree on the logic for the solution. With the logic-first approach, the reviewers may remember some existing logic and suggest that the author reuse it. In a smaller code base where there isn't much existing logic, the reviewers might suggest making a piece of code more generic so other developers can reuse it in the future. Everything other than logic, such as typos and naming conventions, reviewers should note and save for later.

After reviewing the logic, reviewers should pull the code, run tests, and check for errors. After resolving errors, the author should write new tests to cover those error cases. Reviewers should double-check for basic mistakes such as syntax errors and infinite loops. After all tests are passing, the author should revisit earlier feedback for any refactoring suggestions and improvements, such as removing dead code or adding documentation. Before asking for another round of review, the author should also validate their code with the team's code guidelines. Here are some standard things to check:

- Are function and method names clear and descriptive?
- Is the code consistent across different files?
- Do functions accept the same types of parameters and behave the same every time they execute?

At this point, authors who are junior developers might ask their reviewers about ways to optimize and improve code performance if needed.

Once each step has been completed—planning, reviewing logic, fixing bugs, and refactoring—the process is complete and the code is ready to merge.

Appendix A: A coder's vocabulary

Following, in alphabetical order, are some terms that are commonly used among software developers. You may have learned some of them already. Note that these definitions aren't intended to be comprehensive, but rather to help you understand and participate in online and offline conversations about code as quickly as possible. Many of them are based on the most common situations and may not apply to every company or tool (e.g. the definitions relating to version control are specific to Git, the most popular version control system).

Agile - A philosophy for creating and releasing high-quality software gradually (as opposed to Waterfall, where software is delivered all at once). Even though the entirety of the Agile manifesto is available online (https://agilemanifesto.org/[156]) and takes less than ten minutes to read, most people in the technology sector severely misunderstand it or ignore it altogether. If a company says they "do Agile," this generally means that they have a lot of meetings and sell subscriptions to their products, not that they follow Agile principles like valuing simplicity and trusting their developers. Agile is one of the most popular buzzwords in the technology sector.

Algorithm - A set of steps for doing something. An algorithm is the concept that drives a piece of code, not the code itself.

Antipattern - Something that seems like an easy or obvious solution to a problem, but has hidden negative consequences. In other words, "lots of people do this, but it's a bad idea." Be wary of developers who use this to describe any pattern they dislike.

Application Programming Interface (API) - All the parts of a piece of software that are public in a given context - for example, if you're coding something that uses the software, the API is all the parts you can refer to from your own code. The commands in a programming language are part of its API. The methods you import from a third-party library are part of its API. If you write a web server, all the methods that can be accessed via an HTTP request are part of its API. In your own software, every public method and field you create is part of the internal API.

Argument - see "Parameter".

Array - A collection of one or more pieces of data, together in the same group. An array can be as simple as [1, 2, 3] or much more complicated—arrays can contain objects or even other arrays.

Assign - To set or change the value of a variable.

Associative array - See "Object".

Asynchronous (async) - Refers to processes that don't necessarily happen in order and could finish at any time (or not at all). Different coding languages handle this in different ways, but usually

---

[156]https://agilemanifesto.org/

by letting you give them a function to execute when a process is finished, and another function to execute if the process throws an error.

Automated test - A piece of code that executes another piece of code and makes sure it does what it's supposed to do. Automated tests include unit tests, integration tests, and end to end tests, among others.

Back end - The server in a web application. This includes the database and all the server-side code. Many developers specialize in back end development.

Best practice - Any standard that a group of experts have decided is the "best way" to do something. Knowing the best practices of a programming language, framework, or business process can help you develop quickly and avoid expensive mistakes. It's also valuable to know when to ignore a best practice in favor of something that's faster or more practical.

Big O notation - A way of measuring the efficiency of an algorithm, like sorting an array or retrieving data from an object. In Big O notation, O represents a function whose output is the amount of time (or space) it takes to run the algorithm, and n represents the number of items the algorithm is operating on. Since every computer is different, we don't measure in absolute units, but for the following examples I'll use seconds. $O(n)$ could mean "this algorithm will take 1 second to operate on 1 item, 2 seconds to operate on 2 items, 3 seconds to operate on 3 items, and so forth." You can think of it as a line graph, like $y = x$. And $O(2n)$ would mean the algorithm will take two seconds to operate on each item. $O(1)$ would mean the algorithm takes the same exact amount of time regardless of how many items it operates on—this is usually the best case scenario. And $O(n^2)$ would mean the algorithm takes as long as the number of items squared—this is one of the worst case scenarios, since the algorithm will get exponentially slower as the number of items increases linearly.

Blocker - Anything outside of your control that is preventing you from moving forward with your work. Blockers are a common topic of standup meetings.

Branch - One copy of a repository that can be worked on without affecting everyone else's copy. This is managed via version control. When you've finished doing a piece of work in a branch, you merge it back to the main branch (the "trunk"). "Branch" can also refer to a logical possibility in a piece of code—if a piece of code has an "if" statement, one logical branch is the code that executes if the statement is `true`, and the other logical branch is the code that executes if the statement is `false`.

Boolean - A data type that contains either `true` or `false`. A boolean variable is also called a bit or a flag. Booleans are one of the most essential and useful data types.

Bug - When an application doesn't behave the way it's expected to. This is almost always due to a mistake made by a developer while coding the application, or a miscommunication from their manager when describing the requirements for the application. On rare occasions it's due to a deficiency in the programming language itself. Bugs are common and developers learn to expect them in every piece of code. The term "bug" was coined by programming pioneer Grace Hopper, who once traced a malfunction in a computer program to an actual moth trapped in an electromagnetic relay.

Build - A compiled version of a codebase, or the process that compiles it and prepares it for delivery to the user or production server.

Caching - A way of speeding up access to data by storing it in memory. Generally, anything you assign to a variable in code is cached, and retrieving it from that variable is much faster than reading it from a database or a remote API call. Back-end developers tend to use caching liberally, since memory is cheap and cached data scales extremely well.

Character - A letter, number, symbol, space, or other indivisible piece of a string. Some programming languages have a specific data type for characters and represent strings as arrays of characters.

Class - The blueprint or instruction manual for an object. You can use a class to create an object, usually with the new keyword. The class tells you what data the object can hold and what methods it has.

Clean code - Code that has minimal dependencies and is easy to read, well-tested, and error-resistant. Truly clean code is a standard that isn't often achieved in the real world. The best developers strive for this ideal in a pragmatic way, improving existing code while making realistic compromises.

Client - In a web application, the computer on the user's side (as opposed to the server). Can also refer to an application that communicates with another computer over the internet.

Cloud - A general term for computers or servers that are owned by someone else and only accessible via the internet, usually paid for by the consumer on a monthly basis. Your emails and Dropbox files live in the cloud, as do most websites.

Codebase - All the code in a project or repository, or any collection of interconnected files that together form the source code of an application.

Code quality - A measure of the usefulness and readability of a piece of code. See the chapter "Steps to better code".

Code review - When one developer reviews another developer's code and provides feedback.

Code smell - A behavior in code that isn't necessarily wrong, but is an obvious red flag for low-quality code or hidden bugs. For example, a variable named x is a code smell, not because it doesn't work, but because it doesn't describe what the variable contains and could easily be misinterpreted.

Code style - A matter of preference in how code is formatted. Code style includes topics like tabs versus spaces, maximum line length, and bracket placement. Code style doesn't matter much but is still hotly debated on some teams. Ideally, a development team should set up an auto-formatter with rules chosen by any arbitrary method. As a developer, you should conform to the style conventions of whatever team or project you're working in.

Command Line Interface (CLI) - Often called a "console." A CLI is a text interface for using software. The user (often a programmer) types a command and presses Enter, and the software responds and puts the result on the next line. Bash, Powershell, Command Prompt on Windows, and Terminal on Mac are popular examples of CLIs.

Commit - See "Git".

Compile - To transform code into lower-level code, like turning C++ code into machine language. One way or another, this has to be done before the code can execute. Many programming languages come with a compiler that does this transformation quickly and efficiently. Compilation is often done ahead of time, before the software is released to users, but some languages have "JIT" (Just In Time) compilation that happens while the software is being used; still other languages are interpreted rather than compiled (See "Interpret"). Depending on the language and the environment it runs in, a combination of compilation techniques may be used.

Concurrency - When multiple things can happen at once in code.

Constructor - A class method that is called the moment a new object is created. The constructor is usually in charge of assigning default values to the object's fields and setting up its dependencies.

Continuous Integration (CI) - On a software development team, the practice of merging each developer's code to a shared repository frequently and testing it after each merge. Any CI tool on the market will allow you to automatically compile new code and run unit tests on it whenever it is merged, then notify the development team if the tests fail.

Continuous Delivery (CD) - The practice of making sure a piece of software is always ready to release, and releasing it frequently. This requires a little extra work to make sure that half-finished or untested features aren't released by accident. This can be done by hiding unfinished work behind feature flags or by releasing a feature gradually in small but fully-implemented layers.

Convention - Tradition. Programmers speak of "the conventional approach" or "style conventions," by which they mean "the way things have always been done around here." *Here* in this phrase could mean your company, your city, a programming language, or the field of computer science as a whole. Sometimes conventions are a useful shortcut to code and techniques that have stood the test of time; other times, they're obstacles that prevent you from seeing a better way to do things.

Create, Read, Update, Delete (CRUD) - Some of the most common behaviors in interactive applications. A word processor app, for example, will have the ability to Create, Read, Update or Delete documents. An app with little to no logic other than what's required to store and retrieve data is often described as a CRUD app.

Culture fit - This can usually be understood as "someone who looks or talks like us." When a company's culture isn't well defined, this is too often used to shut out job candidates for personal reasons that have no correlation to competence or success in a given role. Using job interviews as a chance to communicate specific cultural values, such as teamwork, inclusion and tactfulness, can reverse these negative effects and produce "culture add" candidates who preserve a company's values while increasing diversity and reducing bias.

Data - Any piece of information that a computer can keep in its memory. Numbers, dates, strings, booleans, and objects are all examples of data.

Database - A set of data stored in memory, usually on a hard drive. Applications almost always have some kind of database where they store data they'll want to use later. For example, an app can store the name and email address of every person who signs up to use it.

Dead code - Code that is unreachable; that is, it can never be executed. For example, if a function is never called, or if code appears after a `return` statement, it's considered dead code. In some cases your IDE will automatically find dead code and bring it to your attention.

Debugging - Finding and fixing bugs in code. Bugs are very common. You should expect to spend far more time debugging code than writing it.

Declare - To give a variable a name (and possibly a type). A variable declaration is like a birth certificate for a piece of data.

Dependency - Anything that is required for a class to be constructed or for an application to run.

Dependency injection - The practice of passing a class's dependencies to it as parameters to the constructor, rather than making it responsible for gathering everything it needs. Dependency injection is a best practice in most programming languages and makes it easier to write unit tests.

Deploy - To move resources from one environment to another. Deploying software is a process that may include moving files to a server, compiling them, and running automated tests. Most companies automate this process to make it predictable and convenient. See also "Release".

Design pattern - A popular way to solve a particular problem in code. These often have odd names like "the decorator pattern" or "the adapter pattern". Sometimes language-specific patterns are called design patterns, but generally a design pattern should be applicable to an entire family or paradigm of languages. As you explore a codebase, you'll notice the patterns that exist in it without necessarily learning their names. It's more important to know what a pattern does and why it's useful than to know what it's called.

Dev - Short for "developer." Someone who develops software, including the work of writing code.

DevOps - An abbreviation combining "development" and "operations". DevOps describes the overlap between development tasks—defining and creating a product—and operations tasks like deploying software to an environment. Someone who works in DevOps will generally have experience in both areas.

Dictionary - See "Object".

Diff - The result of running a "diff tool." A diff tool is a piece of software that compares two code files and displays the differences between them, much like the "View Changes" tool in a word processor. Code that was added will be shown in green and/or with a "+" symbol, while code that was removed will be shown in red and/or with a "-" symbol. Diffing is often done while merging code, to make sure that changes made by different developers are all integrated together correctly.

Documentation - Written instructions, descriptions, or historical records related to a team or a piece of software.

Edge case - Something that's unlikely to happen in a particular application, but should be planned for anyway. For example, the user of an email application could decide to forward an email to themself, and while this isn't something most users will ever do, the application should still be able to handle it without breaking.

Elegant - Code that is well-written, even beautiful. If two pieces of code do the same task and are both performant and bug-free, the more elegant one is the one that is easier to understand or makes better use of the programming language and its standard library. Calling someone's code "elegant" is a compliment. Elegance shouldn't be confused with "cleverness," which can sometimes mean using language features in a confusing way to get shorter or faster code.

Encapsulation - Taking data and logic that belong together and putting them in a self-contained unit of code. This makes it easy to hand them out to any code that wants to use them, and to control the way they are used.

Encryption - The use of a secret cypher to make important data difficult or impossible for hackers to read.

End to end (e2e) test - An automated test that runs an application as if it were a real user, including clicking, tapping, typing, scrolling, or anything else a real user might do. These tests are time-consuming but they're also the only way to ensure the application actually works without testing it manually. For that reason, they tend to provide a lot of value.

Estimating - The practice of trying to guess how long it will take to develop something. These guesses are usually wrong. The more specific a guess is, the less accurate it's likely to be. Nonetheless, managers desperate for control will often try to get developers to give highly specific estimates for all their work.

Evaluate - To execute a piece of code. If the code produces a value, we can say the code "evaluated to" that value.

Expression - A piece of code that produces a value. Expressions can be made of smaller expressions. The number 2 is an expression in code, as is 120 / 1 + 1 and getUserData().

Feature flag - A boolean value that determines whether a feature is visible or usable to the end user. This is useful when a feature isn't finished yet but the current latest version of the code needs to be released. It can be as simple as placing a piece of code inside an if block, or as complex as using different data types across multiple files based on a value in a database.

Flag - See "Boolean".

Foo, bar, baz, qux - Generic, meaningless variable names often used in code samples or documentation. They're equivalent to a, b, c, and d. They shouldn't be used in actual application code.

Framework - A generic piece of software that makes certain common tasks easier; this is meant to be used as the foundation for an application. A web framework, for example, can simplify the work of creating websites by providing methods for updating web pages when data changes, sharing data between pages, and communicating with a web server.

Front end - In a web application, the code that runs on the user's computer (generally a website or an app). The opposite of "back end." Many developers specialize in front end development. Front end development often includes elements of graphic design.

Full stack - Both the front end and the back end in a web application. The term "full stack developer" is contentious because many people believe that a developer can't effectively specialize in both the front end and the back end. However, most web developers know some of both.

Function - One or more lines of code that are grouped together in the same block and share data with each other. A function usually has a name so you can call it from another piece of code. Functions can accept arguments and return values (but they don't have to do either). They're a good way to break down a long process into simpler steps or share logic between several pieces of code.

Functional programming (FP) - A paradigm that describes programming languages or techniques where all data is immutable, all functions are pure, and the core concepts are based on advanced math. Haskell, Elm and F# are examples of functional programming languages. However, a functional programming "style" can be used in many other languages, including JavaScript and C#.

Garbage collection (GC) - A feature in many programming languages that keeps track of data you aren't using anymore and automatically deletes it to free up memory. This is a major convenience for developers. In languages without garbage collection, you have to keep track of all your data and delete it yourself to avoid memory leaks.

Getter - A function that controls what happens when a variable is accessed. Getters are sometimes used to control who can access a variable and what value they receive. The code referring to the variable probably doesn't know that it's calling a function, so getters should be used carefully. See also "Setter".

Git - The most popular version control system. Git keeps track of a series of "commits," each of which is a collection of file changes or "deltas." These commits exist in one or more "branches". When one branch is merged into another, Git tries to take all the changes in each file and weave them together. It often can't figure out how to do so without losing anyone's changes; this results in merge conflicts.

Gotcha - A pitfall. Anything about a programming language, library, design pattern, or apparent solution that can have unexpected effects, often without the developer realizing it.

Hard-coding - When data is written into code as a shortcut, forcing the code to use that data instead of getting it from whatever "real" source it's supposed to use. This is a form of technical debt. It's often done on purpose when building a new app or feature. For example, when you build a new web page, you might hard-code some fake data for it to display (like a username, profile picture, and map location) so you can focus on the design and interface. Every time you load the page, the same fake data will be shown. Once the design work is finished, then you'll need to refactor so that the page uses data from a real logged-in user, maybe by fetching that data from the application's server. Hard-coding can also be called "stubbing."

Graphical User Interface (GUI) - A visual interface for using software, generally accessed with a mouse and keyboard. Ubuntu Linux, Mac OS, and Windows all come with GUIs installed, as does every major internet browser and almost every other application meant for end users.

Idempotent - Describes a method that can be called once, twice, or multiple times, and the result is always the same—that is, it doesn't matter how many times you call it.

Idiomatic - The most obvious or normal way to do something in a programming language. Idiomatic code takes advantage of a language's built-in features and standard library to complete a task in an expectable way, rather than writing unnecessary methods or misusing language features to do something they weren't intended for.

Immutable - Refers to data that can't or shouldn't be altered. A changed version of that data could be created and stored in a different variable, but the original data should always stay the same. Immutable data can be nice to work with because it's unlikely to surprise you.

Infinite loop - A loop, such as a `while` or `for` loop, that has a bug causing it to repeat forever. This often happens when the programmer forgets to increase a value on each iteration, or when the condition of the loop is written incorrectly. `while(true) {}` is an example of an infinite loop.

Integrated development environment (IDE) - A code editor that includes code-specific features, like a compiler, a test runner, a debugger, and/or autocomplete. Visual Studio, IntelliJ, and WebStorm are examples of IDEs.

Integration test - An automated test that makes sure two or more pieces of code work together correctly.

Interface - The way you interact with a piece of code. This can refer to the input boxes and buttons of a Graphical User Interface, the hardware buttons on a microwave, or the public parts of a class. In code, the *interface* keyword is used to describe a collection of public fields and method signatures which describe the interactivity an object is expected to have without specifying the exact logic it should be using under the hood.

Interpret - Refers to the process of executing code without compiling it to machine language first (see "Compile"). This requires a special piece of software called an interpreter. Languages that are interpreted instead of compiled are often called "scripting" languages. JavaScript is an example of an interpreted language; every major web browser comes with a JavaScript interpreter.

It works on my machine - Often said by a developer when an application is broken for the QA team, managers, or users, but doesn't seem to have any issues when they run it on their computer. There are many reasons this can happen, including out-of-date code, a race condition, concurrency bugs, differences in data, differences in environment, unforeseen user behavior, or bugs in the build and delivery system.

Kanban - A set of processes that are often used in software development. Kanban is most easily recognized by the presence of a "Kanban board," a grid representing tasks that are available, in progress, or finished, often with intermediate steps in between. See also "Scrum" and "Agile".

Keyword - See "Reserved word".

Legacy code - Any code that no longer brings joy to the developers that maintain it. Legacy code may have been written ten years ago or last week; the point of the phrase isn't necessarily to describe the code's age, but to indicate that it's obsolete in some way and needs to be updated.

Library - See "Package". Can also refer to a collection of related packages.

Linter - A tool that detects style issues or common mistakes in code without actually compiling or running it. Linting is a form of static analysis.

Load test - An automated test that simulates heavy usage of an application (e.g. by a lot of different users at the same time). The goal is to measure the performance of the application "under load," or in other words, to find out how much it slows down or stops working in worst case scenarios.

Logic - What an application does or how it makes decisions.

Memory - See "Random access memory".

Memory leak - When an application fails to free up memory it doesn't need anymore, it can gradually use more and more memory until the computer runs out. This can happen in any programming language, whether or not it has garbage collection.

Merge - See "Git".

Merge conflict - When two developers have modified the same code and the version control system can't figure out how to weave their changes together, the result is a merge conflict. A developer then needs to resolve the conflict, usually by opening the file and modifying it so neither developer's work is lost.

Method - A function that lives inside of an object. It's often defined in a class.

Minimum viable product (MVP) - The smallest and simplest version of a software product or feature that could be valuable to a user. Releasing an MVP is a good way to find out what's important to users and learn about their needs without a lot of development effort.

Mob programming - Often called "mobbing". When more than two developers gather around a single computer and focus on a single task, with the entire group contributing to discussion about how to do it.

Mock - A "fake" version of a dependency (like an object or method) that can be used during unit testing, so the test won't fail for reasons outside of the piece of code being tested.

Mockup - See "Prototype".

Modular - Refers to a piece of code that is self-contained, making it portable between codebases.

Module - See "Package".

Monitoring - Use of a system that keeps track of different events and metrics for an application. You can use monitoring to learn what kinds of errors are happening for your users or how fast or slow your app is. Monitoring can also notify you when a server crashes or a database takes too long to perform an operation.

Mutable - Refers to data that can be altered. The opposite of immutable.

Namespace - A name that groups one or more pieces of code together under the same umbrella for the programmer's convenience. Some programming languages require every class to be in a namespace. When one class refers to another, you can use its namespace to help the compiler find it, or to differentiate between multiple classes with the same name.

Object - A piece of data that holds other pieces of data and/or logic. Organizing data like this is a good way to describe a complicated real-world concept, like a person or a subscription. Objects are usually organized into keys and values. The keys are like words in a real-life dictionary; the values are like the definitions of those words. Therefore, you use the keys (which you usually know beforehand) to retrieve the values from the object or to change them. An object can be created by using a class. Objects can also be called dictionaries or associative arrays.

Object-oriented programming (OOP) - A paradigm that describes programming languages where the code is organized around mutable data objects. OOP languages generally use classes and each class has methods for operating on its own data.

Open source - Describes a project or application whose code is publicly available. Open source coding is extremely popular, and tens of millions of open source repositories can be found on sites like GitHub and BitBucket. Developers value open source code because of the communities that form around it, the way it propagates ideas, the transparency it offers, and the fact that most open source code is free to use.

Package - A bundle of code intended to be used by other code. A package may depend on other packages, but it usually handles those dependencies on its own. In the simplest situations, you can add a package to your project and use it without worrying about how it works.

Pair programming - When two developers share a computer. One of them, the "driver", controls the mouse and keyboard; the other one tells them what to do or type. The goal is to reduce mistakes and increase development speed by having two people focused on the same task.

Paradigm - A category of programming language, or a certain way of programming regardless of language. Functional programming and object-oriented programming are examples of paradigms.

Parameter - A piece of data you provide to a function when you call it. It's assumed that the function will use and/or alter that data.

Performance - How fast or slow an application or part of an application is. Something that's relatively fast is called "performant."

Premature optimization - When someone tries to make an application faster without knowing how fast it is already. Most of the time, "fast enough" is good enough. Almost any piece of code can be fine-tuned and worked over until it's lightning-fast, but this is wasted effort if a user will never notice the difference.

Primitive - A simple, "pure" data type that isn't an object. What's considered a "primitive" can vary by programming language. Numbers, booleans and characters are usually primitives.

Production - In a web application, the server that is interacting with real users. This is the last stop for any piece of code that's been merged into the main branch.

Proof of Concept (PoC) - A small example of working software to demonstrate that a particular idea or technique is feasible.

Prototype - An application design that represents both the appearance and the interactivity of the app, usually put together by a designer. Usually a prototype is purely visual and doesn't contain any code or do any work under the hood.

Pseudocode - Fake code written as an example or to describe how an algorithm might be written. Pseudocode may look like a specific programming language or no programming language at all. Many programmers like to write pseudocode when planning their approach to a problem, so they can figure out the solution without worrying about syntax, spelling, code style, and errors.

Pull request (PR) - In version control, a proposal for one branch to be merged into another. A pull request usually includes a written description of the changes the developer has made and a list of all the commits that would need to be applied. Most online code repositories have a way to read through all the code changes that a pull request is proposing, and a method for approving or rejecting the request.

Pure function - A function that doesn't change anything outside of itself and doesn't use any data aside from its arguments. A function that accepts a Fahrenheit value and returns the equivalent Celsius value, doing the conversion with a simple mathematical formula, is an example of a pure function. Pure functions are easy to use and very predictable, which makes them a useful tool for any developer.

Quality assurance (QA) - Testing software to find bugs. Depending on the organization, this can be a person or team's full-time job, or a responsibility shared by everyone. It's an extremely valuable role that often prevents catastrophic bugs from affecting users.

Race condition - A bug that occurs when two or more things happen at the same time and are expected to finish in a certain order, but might not. Race conditions are common in asynchronous code and in web applications that expect data to be delivered from the server in a particular order.

Random access memory (RAM) - Often just called "memory". The place where the computer stores data temporarily. RAM is very fast and easy to access. All variables in a computer program are stored in RAM.

Read–eval–print loop (REPL) - See also "Command Line Interface". A text interface for evaluating expressions in a programming language. Most languages ship with a REPL. The developer console in Chrome, Firefox and Safari includes a JavaScript REPL.

Read the fucking manual (RTFM) - An abusive way to suggest that someone is asking an excessively simple question, and instead of bothering you they should read the documentation for the programming language or tool they're struggling with. RTFM is an unhelpful response regardless of the situation, and generally only used by people who are exceptionally difficult to work with.

Recursion - When a function calls itself. This is often done when a function is working with data like an array or tree of indefinite length or depth. The function can operate on the first part of the data, then call itself with the rest of the data. Eventually it will be called with the last piece of data, and then it can finish.

Refactor - To change a piece of code without changing how the application behaves on the surface. The purpose of refactoring can be to make code easier to read, to organize it better, to make it easier to add new behavior in the future, or to take advantage of new features in a programming language or library.

Reference - The memory address of a variable. When you create a variable and use it, the code is keeping track of its reference (usually behind the scenes). If you delete the variable or the compiler notices you're not using it anymore, it can "free" the reference so that memory can be used by something else. If something is "passed by reference" to a function, that means its actual memory address is provided, so modifying it within the function will modify it for the entire application.

Reflection - The ability of code to modify itself at runtime. In practical terms, this usually refers to the ability in certain programming languages to look at an object and access any of its fields and methods that are created at runtime or would usually be hidden. This is especially useful if you don't know what the object is going to look like ahead of time.

Relational database - A database consisting of tables that can refer to each other. You can think of a database table like a spreadsheet. It commonly has an ID column and other columns that describe a complex piece of data; in this way the table definition (or "schema") is like a class and each row is like an object of that class. If you have a table called "Orders" and a table called "Products", the "Orders" table could have a "ProductID" column that refers to the ID column of "Products". Then each order could be related to a product (usually by using the numerical ID of a single row). Relational databases are the best choice for most applications. Most relational databases are created, queried and updated via SQL, a programming language made for this purpose.

Release - To publish code to an environment, usually production; or, a version of code that is ready to be released.

Repository - A collection of files that are all kept in the same place. Often abbreviated to "repo".

Reserved word - In a given programming language, any word that has special meaning and therefore can't be used for variable or function names. For example, the word if is usually a reserved word, and if you try to declare a variable named if you'll get an error.

Representational state transfer (REST) - By strict definition, this is a set of rules for web server APIs that dictates, among other things, how APIs are structured and what information the client must provide. In common usage, a REST API is any web API that uses common HTTP request bodies and HTTP verbs like GET, POST and PUT.

Retrospective - A meeting during which developers and managers consider the work they've done recently and discuss ways to improve. This is the only meeting that is actually part of Agile: "At regular intervals, the team reflects on how to become more effective, then tunes and adjusts its behavior accordingly." (https://agilemanifesto.org/principles.html[157])

Rollback - A process by which a piece of software is "un-updated"; any changes in the latest release are undone and the software reverts to an older state. This is usually done when a severe bug or security flaw that didn't exist in previous versions is discovered. Software companies generally plan for this possibility by (for example) setting up an automated way to do a rollback with a single click.

Rubber ducking - The practice of explaining a problem to an inanimate object (it's called a "rubber duck" for illustrative purposes). As you describe the issue out loud in your own words, the solution will often become obvious. This is an especially effective tool for debugging.

---

[157]https://agilemanifesto.org/principles.html

Runtime - The time during which the code is actually running (not being written or compiled); or, the environment in which the code runs.

Scaling - A set of strategies and considerations around the question, "how could our application or organization handle a significant increase in the number of customers we serve?" Scaling can also refer to challenges with increasing amounts of data or organizational growth.

Schema - See "Relational database".

Scope - The boundary between what you intend to build and what you don't intend to build. If you're planning to build a feature in a certain period of time, that feature is "in scope." Otherwise it's "out of scope." If you've already made plans but extenuating circumstances cause you to do more work than you were planning, that's called "scope creep."

Scrum - A set of meetings and processes that are a popular way to "do Agile." The most common mark of Scrum is the "standup", a daily meeting where members of a team report what they're working on. Some organizations wrongly believe that they are Agile solely because they have sprints and standup; see "Agile".

Setter - A function that controls what happens when a variable is changed. A setter can be used to track changes to a variable, prevent it from being changed, or determine if the user has permission to change it. The code referring to this variable probably doesn't know that it's calling a function, so setters should be used carefully. See also "Getter".

Ship - To release a version of a product, usually the latest version.

Signature - Everything you need to know in order to use a method: its name, the types of arguments it expects, and what type of argument it returns.

Soft skills - Refers to non-technical skills that are essential in the workplace, like communication, respectfulness, compromise, time management, and creativity. The phrase has some unfortunate connotations, like wrongly implying that "soft" skills are less important than "hard" (technical) skills, or that they're a sign of intellectual weakness. Many programmers prefer to call them "catalytic skills," since they enable and facilitate every kind of work.

Software - Applications built with code that run on a computer.

Software as a Service (SaaS) - A way of delivering software on a subscription basis. Customers usually pay monthly and receive regular, automatic updates. SaaS is a popular way to sell software on the internet.

Software development kit (SDK) - The software and APIs necessary to develop an application that works on a particular platform, like Windows 10, iPhone, or the Java Virtual Machine (JVM).

SOLID - An acronym for five principles that are common in the study of object-oriented programming: Single responsibility principle, Open-closed principle, Liskov substitution principle, Interface segregation principle, and Dependency inversion principle. These aren't defined here because some of them are relatively advanced, but you should study them once you feel confident with the basics of object-oriented programming.

Spaghetti code - Code that is disorganized, spread out, and hard to follow, as if the code were noodles in a bowl of spaghetti. Developers who are in a rush to meet deadlines or don't have the guidance of a senior developer will often produce spaghetti code. An application made of spaghetti code is a nightmare to debug, refactor, and build upon. Be wary of developers who use the term to describe any code they dislike.

Specification - A detailed human-language description of a software or programming language feature, including details on how it works and how to use it.

Sprint - A period of time during which software is built. The Agile principles state, "Deliver working software frequently, from a couple of weeks to a couple of months, with a preference to the shorter timescale" (https://agilemanifesto.org/principles.html[158]). Sprints are a popular implementation of this principle. A sprint often begins with a planning meeting and ends with a retrospective.

Stack - A memory structure where pieces of data are "stacked" on top of each other. Only the top piece of the stack can be accessed or removed at any given time. The "stack" also refers to all the lines of code that are active when a specific line of code is executed. If code A calls code B, which calls code C, then A, B and C are all part of the stack. If C throws an error, you'll usually see a "stack trace" listing C, then B, then A.

Staging - The environment where an application is released before it goes to production. Staging is where all the final testing and verification happens and often has similar data to production. If a bug isn't caught in staging, it will go to production and affect users.

Standard library - All the functionality that comes built-in with a programming language, even though it isn't part of the syntax itself. The standard library usually includes functions for manipulating strings, handling input and output, and doing advanced math.

Standup - See "Scrum".

State - The data kept in memory as an application runs.

Statement - A basic unit of code that describes an action. In programming, we often talk about "if statements," "return statements," and several others. An "if statement" is a statement that uses the `if` keyword, such as `if (x == 2)`.

Static - A keyword in many programming languages that refers to a method or field that exists on the class itself, not on objects of that class.

Static analysis - A type of debugging that can be done without compiling or running the code. Linting is a form of static analysis. Most IDEs will do static analysis to let you know about bugs as soon as possible.

String - A data type that holds text. In code, strings are usually put inside of quotes. `"John Smith"` is a string, as is `" "` (a string full of spaces), `""` (an empty string) and `"▯"`.

Style guide - A set of rules documenting a group or project's preferred code style. Some teams have unwritten style guides; in this case, the best thing to do is explore the project beforehand and try to make your code look like theirs.

---

[158]https://agilemanifesto.org/principles.html

Syntax - The grammar of a programming language, including all its reserved words and the way numbers, symbols, and other tokens are used.

Technical debt - The gradual buildup of confusing, disorganized or buggy code in an application. This is inevitable over time, especially if the team is rushed, the work environment is hostile, or there's a lot of pressure to produce new features. Technical debt can only be controlled by regularly setting aside development time to refactor. If technical debt is allowed to grow too large, it can cause mental exhaustion for developers, seriously slow down feature development, and make bugs hard or impossible to fix.

Test-driven development (TDD) - The practice of writing unit tests for a piece of code before that code is even written. The process can be remembered as "red-green-refactor": first the test is written, and it fails (red) because no code has been written. Then code is implemented so that the test passes (green). Then the code can be refactored to improve quality.

Throw - If a piece of code runs into an error it can't or shouldn't handle on its own, it can throw the error (or do nothing, in which case the error will usually be thrown automatically). Then the code that called it will receive the error. That code can also handle, throw, or ignore the error. If the error is thrown enough times, it can reach the user.

Type - The kind of data stored in a variable, e.g. a whole number, a decimal number, a boolean, a string, or an object.

Unicorn - A privately-held tech company whose total stock value is over one billion dollars. Sometimes this word is also used to indicate something incredibly rare and precious, like certain types of developers.

Unit test - An automated test that makes sure a single, isolated piece of code (like a class or method) does what it's expected to do. Unit tests usually run very quickly and can help build confidence in a tricky piece of code. The best unit tests verify a unit's behavior, not its implementation—that is, they test *what* it does, not *how* it does it. This way the code can be refactored without breaking the test.

Usability testing - The practice of having someone (usually a person from outside of the team or company) use an application or prototype while a member of the team watches. Ideally, the team member shouldn't tell the person *how* to do anything; instead, they should give them an objective and see if they can figure out how to complete it in the application. This helps the team understand what parts of the application are confusing or unintuitive.

User interface (UI) - The part of an application that a user looks at and interacts with; or, the work of designing this part of an application, often done by a graphic designer or someone with artistic training.

User experience (UX) - The field of study focused on improving the interactions between users and applications. UX designers may build prototypes or design interfaces, but they're generally more concerned with usefulness and user-friendliness than with appearance.

Value - A piece of data. If we say something is "passed by value" to a function, then we mean the data itself is provided, not the memory address of the variable that holds it. This way the function can modify it without affecting the rest of the application.

Variable - A named piece of data in memory. In the statement int x = 1, the variable is x.

Velocity - A measure of development speed based on estimates. Velocity is generally impossible to measure in a useful way. Incompetent managers often try to increase velocity by making developers work longer hours and meet shorter deadlines; this always results in a worse product and long-term damage to the company.

Version control system (VCS) - A system for managing several different versions of a codebase. Usually there is a main or "master" branch which contains the latest and most official version of the code, and then several other branches containing work in progress. These other branches can be merged into the master branch when they're complete.

Vulnerability - A weakness or bug in an application that hackers could use to steal user data, crash the application, or gain unauthorized access. Vulnerabilities can be avoided through the use of security best practices, encryption, input sanitization, and penetration testing.

Waterfall - A development process for software that is delivered all at once, like on a CD. This was popular in the days before the internet became the primary medium for software distribution. In Waterfall, planning and design are all done at the beginning of the project, which can make the process inflexible and prone to error.

Whiteboard interview - A popular but ineffective interview method where candidates are asked to write code on a whiteboard, chalkboard or sheet of paper. This often includes asking them to solve complex mathematical or data structure problems with code. Since this doesn't resemble the work they'd be doing on a day-to-day basis if they were hired, it's almost irrelevant to the task of selecting the most competent candidate.

Workaround - A less-than-ideal way to work when some issue makes the normal way impossible. If the "Send" button on your email client is broken, but pressing Ctrl + Enter sends the email, that's a workaround. You can continue to use the software, but it definitely needs to be fixed.

XY Problem - When a user has a problem ("X"), thinks they know the solution ("Y"), and asks for help with that solution ("Y") instead of the original problem ("X"). People sometimes do this to avoid looking naive ("I have a problem but no idea how to solve it" can be a hard thing to say), or because they think asking about Y is a smaller or less intrusive question. Sometimes they may not even recognize that X is their real problem. This often results in confusion and frustration, especially when the user's Y isn't a good solution to X (or isn't even related to it). For example, suppose your computer won't turn on and you decide—for good reasons or bad ones—that the problem is the power cord. You might call a friend who's good with computers and ask them where to buy a new cord. If you're lucky, they'll ask some broader questions and find out what's really going on. If not, you may find out the hard way that a new cord doesn't solve the problem, and lose a lot of time and money in the process.

Appendix B: To make this, learn that

Deciding what to learn can be easier if you know what you want to build. To that end, below are some things you might be interested in building and some of the most popular tools used to make them. Note that this isn't a complete or comprehensive list—there are many more things a developer can make and many tools used to make them.

To make this	Learn that
Android apps	Java *or* Kotlin; Android Studio
Cross-platform apps	C# and Xamarin *or* HTML, CSS, JavaScript and Phonegap *or* a front-end framework and Ionic *or* Dart and Flutter *or* a front-end framework and NativeScript
Embedded systems, like ATM machines, gas pumps and credit card readers	C *or* C++
iOS apps	Swift *or* Objective-C; Xcode
Video games	C# and Unity *or* C++ and Unreal Engine *or* Lua and Amazon Lumberyard
Web apps	HTML; CSS; SASS *or* LESS; JavaScript; Vue *or* React *or* Ember; Webpack *or* Rollup; TypeScript
Web servers	C# and .NET Framework *or* JavaScript and Node.js *or* Python and Django *or* Erlang and Elixir *or* Ruby and Rails *or* PHP and Laravel

Appendix C: Recommended reading

Code Complete by Steve McConnell. A several-hundred-page deep-dive on how to write clean, bug-free code.

CSS-Tricks (https://css-tricks.com/[159]). A website offering simple and extremely well-written guides for many different web development topics (not just CSS).

Emotional Intelligence for Engineers by April Wensel (https://www.youtube.com/watch?v=yD0kzU4Pu-Q[160]). A discussion of oft-neglected but incredibly important skills in software development.

#firstyearincode on The DEV Community (https://dev.to/t/firstyearincode[161]). A collection of posts related to this book. May include book reviews, chapters from the book, unpublished chapters, and more.

How to Manage Conflicts by Isaac Lee (https://dev.to/ijlee2/how-to-manage-conflicts-listen-4kmb[162]). A three-part series about effective teamwork, applying the principles of Crucial Conversations to software development.

How to Think Like a Computer Scientist by Allen Downey, Jeffrey Elkner and Chris Meyers. A very good how-to-code guide for beginners using the Python language.

It Doesn't Have to be Crazy at Work by David Heinemeier Hansson and Jason Fried. A manifesto for running a business, especially a software business, in a sensible way that respects employees and clients.

Learn You a Haskell for Great Good! by Miran Lipovaca. An introduction to functional programming with the Haskell programming language.

MDN Web Docs by Mozilla (https://developer.mozilla.org[163]). The web's most well-maintained and up-to-date source for information about web technologies, including complete documentation for HTML, CSS, JavaScript, and browser APIs.

The Nature of Software Development by Ron Jeffries. A brief overview of how Agile principles can be applied to a real-world development team.

Refactoring UI by Adam Wathan and Steve Schoger. A brief introduction to the rules of good user interface design, written for software developers.

SOLID on Wikipedia (https://en.wikipedia.org/wiki/SOLID[164]). A starting point for learning about the most famous principles of good object-oriented code.

---

[159] https://css-tricks.com/
[160] https://www.youtube.com/watch?v=yD0kzU4Pu-Q
[161] https://dev.to/t/firstyearincode
[162] https://dev.to/ijlee2/how-to-manage-conflicts-listen-4kmb
[163] https://developer.mozilla.org
[164] https://en.wikipedia.org/wiki/SOLID

Structure and Interpretation of Computer Programs by Harold Abelson, Gerald Jay Sussman and Julie Sussman. A classic computer programming manual used at MIT. The full text is available online at https://mitpress.mit.edu/sites/default/files/sicp/index.html[165].

Three Virtues by Larry Wall (http://threevirtues.com/[166]). A summary of the tongue-in-cheek "great virtues" of a programmer: laziness, impatience, and hubris.

---

[165]https://mitpress.mit.edu/sites/default/files/sicp/index.html
[166]http://threevirtues.com/

Acknowledgments

Thanks to everyone who supported this book. It was very much a group effort, and it's been amazing to work with all of you.

Thanks to the wonderful DEV Community[167] team for their help organizing and promoting the book.

Thanks to Dylan for your support during long hours of writing and editing. Love you always.

Each of our contributors and beta readers has written a brief message, which you can read below.

Guest authors

I am very thankful to Isaac Lyman for giving us this opportunity to contribute in this great book. Find more about me @ arslanaslam.me

~ *Muhammad Arslan Aslam*

My name is Ilona and I am a Frontend Software Engineer based in Berlin. I develop web apps, study psychology and help #womenwhocode live a life they don't need a vacation from. Read my blog at ilonacodes.com and say "Hi" on Twitter: @ilonacodes

~ *Ilona Codes*

I am a web application developer and passionate about functional programming and open source. Having multiple side projects going on at the same while trying to fulfill my entrepreneurial dreams... :) Follow me on Twitter @leonorader and check my blog: https://fejlesztolany.hu

~ *Leonóra Dér*

Thank you mom, dad & friends for your support & Isaac Lyman for this opportunity to help contribute to an amazing cause.

Readers: if you have questions or would like to follow my new journey as I build my new company (rawpido.com), connect with me at cliffordfajardo.com

~ *Clifford Fajardo*

Hi, I'm Gianluca Fiore, a software developer from Italy. On the spare time between tasting coffee, making pizza, travelling, blogging (on https://papersounds.eu) and reading, I actually do develop software (mostly in Python, Go and JS).

~ *Gianluca Fiore*

---

[167]https://dev.to

I would like to thank Kieran for believing in me and supporting me when life felt too heavy. Thank you for always encouraging me to take the next step.

~ *Sabrina Gannon*

I would tell you a UDP joke, but you may not get it. I am a passionate software engineer, dedicated to continuous personal/professional improvement and in the meanwhile, I am torturing people with my jokes. I am glad to assist you in your first year in code.

~ *Periklis Gkolias*

I'm a career changer and bootcamp grad. I was helped along the way by so many awesome people and I'm always trying to pay it forward. Please feel free to reach out!

~ *Yechiel Kalmenson*

"Simple things should be simple, complex things should be possible." - Alan Kay

~ *Vlad Levin*

Thank you for joining the fabulous world of programming. Let's keep it rich and interesting, as my own career has been.

Check out my book, "What is Programming?" a further companion to your journey as a programmer.

Find me at https://edaqa.com/

~ *Edaqa Mortoray*

During the moments of time where there are crucial decisions to be made, often you already know what path you feel is the right one to take. I urge you to trust your gut. It's the one true compass you can always count on. Trust your compass.

~ *Connor Ocampo*

I run my life with three words: Build, Test, Launch.

~ *Rosalind Thuy Pham*

Hi, I'm Desi! I love UX research, finding bugs, and helping people find their dream jobs. I'm on Twitter @desilove and my portfolio is www.desidoes.dev. Special thanks to my partner, Evan, for relentless editing of chapter drafts!

~ *Desi Rottman*

A programmer and entrepreneur with a love of cars, music and technology. https://turnerj.com/

~*James Turner*

I live in Utah and am currently a Senior Software Engineer at GoReact. I have been programming as a hobby since 2009, professionally since 2012. I've contributed to the community through open source, blog posts garnering over 100,000 reads, as well as presenting at meetups.

~ *John Woodruff*

Beta readers

I am Mohammed and I am a Software Developer. I am passionate about social media analytics and mentoring new or aspiring developers. Special thanks to Isaac Lyman for the opportunity to participate in this interesting book. Please feel free to follow me on Twitter @MohammedAlMarh

~ *Mohammed Almarhoon*

Hi there! I love learning about Web Development, drawing and doing a little bit of exercise - just a bit! -. I'll definitely use what I learned with the book to enter the Dev arena and improve this https://github.com/john-angel. See ya!

~ *John Angel*

Hi, I'm Glenn, an android developer from Belgium and a huge open source fan. Checkout my blog posts and projects on https://glennmen.dev

~ *Glenn Carremans*

I'm a Software Engineer, Entrepreneur and Investor. You'll find all of my contact info at http://www.jeremiahcooper.com. Feel free to reach out if you think we can work together on something.

~ *Jeremiah Cooper*

I'm a self-taught email & front-end developer. I am passionate about open source software and encouraging developers to participate. I can be found Tweeting about tech (https://twitter.com/shannon_crabill) or speaking at conferences. My internet home is http://shannoncrabill.com.

~ *Shannon Crabill*

I am a full stack web developer who loves learning and sharing knowledge. Firmly believe "life is a marathon, not a sprint". I enjoy sharing web development knowledge on a website I run called dev-diaries.com

~ *Khaliq Gant*

FOR x equals one to ten;

Loop and do it again;

Not sure what to write, I truly am vexed;

This BASIC loop ends with a NEXT.

Doug is a coder, leader, innovator, and teacher. Engage with him at http://www.dougjenkinson.net.

~ Doug Jenkinson

I appreciate to Isaac Lyman, all the authors, and big thank you to Jiyoon. I'm working at Emotion AI company, "GenesisLab" from South Korea who started a career 2.5 years ago. I want to say to me in 2009 (when I started). "Please find Isaac and ask him to write this."

~ Junhong Kim

Shoutout to Udacity and all the awesome people at Sovos who have helped me break into software engineering, especially Dirk Diegnau!

Thinking about ordering pork online from from a small farm in Minnesota? I got you covered! tfponline.squarespace.com

ericmiller.dev

@TFP_eric

~ Eric C. Miller, PhD

I am a Tech Writer and YouTuber who explains technology for a living!

~ Amruta Ranade

Thank you Isaac from your help and your support to the community, specially to newbies like me and also to the authors who beautifully contributed to this great guide.

~ Adrian Skar

https://sysa.la

~ Jan Sysala

Cover design

Cover art created by Cover Story Book Design. Email us at coverstorybookdesign@gmail.com for your own custom book cover, or to browse our gallery of premade ebook covers! We design for all genres, fiction and nonfiction.

CPSIA information can be obtained
at www.ICGtesting.com
Printed in the USA
BVHW012312091019

560429BV00062B/929/P

9 780578 564999